THE REBEL
DIET

THE REBEL DIET

BENJI XAVIER

Publisher Mike Sanders
Art & Design Director William Thomas
Editorial Director Ann Barton
Senior Editor Brook Farling
Designer Studio Noel
Food Photographer Daniel Showalter
Food Stylist Lovoni Walker
Chef Ashley Brooks
Recipe Tester Lovoni Walker
Cover and Lifestyle Photographer Dan Heinkel
Cover and Lifestyle Stylist Jenn Friberg
Copy Editor Claire Safran
Proofreaders Claire Safran and Monica Stone
Indexer Michael Goldstein

First American Edition, 2024
Published in the United States by DK Publishing
1745 Broadway, 20th Floor, New York, NY 10019

The authorized representative in the EEA is Dorling
Kindersley Verlag GmbH. Arnulfstr. 124, 80636 Munich,
Germany

A catalog record for this book
is available from the Library of Congress.
ISBN 978-0-5938-4960-6

DK books are available at special discounts when purchased
in bulk for sales promotions, premiums, fund-raising, or
educational use. For details, contact SpecialSales@dk.com

Printed and bound in China

www.dk.com

This book was made with Forest
Stewardship Council™ certified
paper – one small step in DK's
commitment to a sustainable future.
Learn more at
www.dk.com/uk/information/sustainability

To my supporters: thank you for all your constant love and support.

To my biggest cheerleaders:
my mom, dad, and sister.

CONTENTS

INTRODUCTION

Welcome to *The Rebel Diet,* where we break all the rules that you thought you knew about dieting. In a world dominated by restrictive meal plans and tasteless "diet" foods, this book is here to revolutionize your approach to healthy eating. Forget all those toxic diet culture rules, like avoiding indulgent flavors or carbs and only sticking to eating bland salads and vegetables. This cookbook is your guide to savoring the unexpected and delicious on your journey to a healthier you.

Inside these pages, you'll find a collection of recipes that defy conventional diet wisdom. We're celebrating foods often dismissed in the world of weight loss—think creamy avocados, rich dark chocolate, cheese, hearty potatoes, and even bacon. The Rebel Diet isn't about deprivation; it's about redefining your relationship with food and discovering that indulgence can coexist with wellness.

I've always struggled with my weight, and in the past, I kept falling into the trap of following fad and crash diets out of my desperation to lose weight. After many failures, I knew I needed to try something different. This time, when I started my weight loss journey, I knew that I needed to do it in a sustainable and healthy way. I felt that I was rebelling against the toxic diet culture that so many of us fall victim to by refusing to cut out entire food groups or starving myself to achieve weight loss. This is why I named this book *The Rebel Diet.* This cookbook is a collection of recipes that I ate on my weight-loss journey and I've never shared, as well as other lower-calorie recipes that I love.

Whether you're a seasoned chef or a kitchen novice, my cookbook offers something for everyone. From breakfast to dessert, I've got you covered with dishes that are both rebellious and nourishing. It's time discard the old diet dogmas and embrace a new way of eating that is adventurous, sustainable, and delicious.

So welcome to the revolution, where you're going to enjoy every bite on your health journey.

INTROD

CHAPTER 1

VCTION

MY
STORY

I've always been a huge foodie. In fact, my family is full of foodies; the love of food runs in my family, but so does obesity. I started slowly gaining weight as a child, and by the time I was a teenager, I weighed almost 300 pounds. I got a gym membership with my dad. We would work out regularly, and I would try every crash diet under the sun. But I was never really successful—my diets would only last a couple of days and then I would promise myself I would start right back up again the following Monday. I would find myself in this vicious and unsuccessful cycle of torture for most of my preteen and teenage years. It wasn't until I was a freshman in high school that I was able to actually stick to a diet and lose weight. That was the first time I lost 100 pounds. My mom has always been a wonderful home cook, but up to that point, I had only been exposed to my mom's home-cooked Latin meals and American fast food. She had no idea how to cook healthy meals, aside from grilled chicken and steamed vegetables. (You can imagine that wasn't the most appealing meal option for a teenager.) I felt the pressure of being in high school and longing to fit in, so that gave me the determination to push through every obstacle during my first major weight loss. I took matters into my own hands and started learning how to cook healthier meals. I didn't know what I was doing for the most part, but I was having fun discovering new foods that I had never had before.

I kept the weight off by eating healthy and working out throughout the rest of my high school years and most of my college years. That is, until my senior year of college, when I found myself extremely stressed, which ultimately affected my mental health. I started eating fast food to cope with my emotions. It was easier to buy fast food because of my busy schedule, and it also made me feel momentarily happy. I was consuming high-calorie foods from breakfast to dinner every single day, and I started to slowly gain weight again. I graduated with a bachelor's degree in biology in December 2019 and started working as a biologist for a grand total of 1 month before the infamous Covid-19 pandemic shut down the world in March 2020. My mental health only worsened during the lockdown so, of course, I continued to turn to my only source of happiness: food. I was rapidly gaining weight, as I was doing nothing but eating and scrolling through my phone. As the months passed, I completely lost control and didn't care about watching my weight or about my health, I was too preoccupied with the newest social media platform that had taken the world by storm: TikTok. I was locked in, and with nothing but time, all I did was eat and post videos to TikTok. With time, I grew a massive following on the platform from posting comedy-style skits. Creating the comedy videos was a creative outlet for me during a tough time, but I was never passionate about it, and with time, I became extremely embarrassed to be presenting myself in a light that was so different from who I truly am.

By summer of 2021, I had eaten myself back up to almost 300 pounds—AGAIN! I kept having to buy larger and larger clothing, as nothing I owned fit. Finding myself at the same weight I was when I lost my first 100 pounds, I was finally snapped back to reality. I realized how big and unhappy I was, and I wanted to take control of my life again. Finding myself at the same place I was as a teenager really motivated me to get my life together again, so I signed up for the gym and started shopping for healthier foods. I didn't really have a plan at first, but this time, I knew I couldn't start a diet that was restrictive and unrealistic. When I started my second weight-loss journey, I quickly fell in love with the world of health and wellness. I started exploring new healthy recipes and getting experimental in the kitchen again.

I was losing weight and my audience was taking notice. I would see comments asking if I had lost weight or what I was doing to lose weight, but I never publicly addressed it because, at that time, I never shared anything personal online. With my newfound happiness and lifestyle, I promised myself I wouldn't continue to do things that were making me unhappy, so I decided that I no longer was going to make the comedy-style videos I had grown to dislike. I realized I had to put my mental health first, and from that point, I decided I was only going to post content that I was actually passionate about and proud of. In May 2023, I posted my first salad recipe video and, to my surprise, it went viral. I was relieved because I really thought no one would care—I thought people would be upset that I was posting something other than a comedy skit. My comments were flooded with people asking for more recipes, so the next day I shared another recipe, and that video went even more viral than the first! I continued sharing recipes from my weight-loss journey, and my social media platforms continued to grow.

I studied biology in college because it was my intention at the time to enter medical school—I've always felt that my calling in life is to help people. Never did I imagine I was going to be able to do that through social media. I receive tons of messages and comments daily from people telling me about their weight-loss success because of my recipes, and nothing makes me feel more fulfilled than knowing that I am able to help so many people.

HOW THE DIET WORKS

The concept of *The Rebel Diet* is simple: You eat foods that are less calorie dense, so you'll feel satisfied, but you won't be restricting yourself to tiny portions. It's centered around the idea that you do not have to suffer, eliminate entire food groups, demonize food, or starve yourself in order to achieve weight loss. It's about building a healthy relationship with food that ultimately leads to weight loss. There is a misconception that losing weight and eating healthy have to be boring or difficult, but they don't have to be those things at all. You can still have all the foods you love. You can enjoy foods like rice, potatoes, bread, and burgers when they're eaten in moderation and the recipes they're in are made healthier. Why does this eating style work for weight loss? Because you will actually be enjoying what you're eating and also getting full, all while still being in a calorie deficit. Being in a calorie deficit simply means you are burning more calories than you are consuming on a daily basis. Enjoying what you are eating is one of the most

important components of a weight-loss journey because it gives you the mental fortitude to continue on your journey and to not make you feel like you are restricted and suffering. The feelings of restriction and misery that come with crash and fad diets are the reason why they never work in the long term. I've learned that I can still make delicious recipes that don't taste like "diet" food and still feel satiated. Ultimately, *The Rebel Diet* isn't really a diet at all—it's a lifestyle.

Aim for a Calorie Deficit

I often see people being overly concerned about working out and prioritizing it over what they are eating. (Working out is a great tool that absolutely will help you on your weight-loss journey, but you will never be able to outrun an entire pizza.) What you eat, how much of it you eat, and remaining in a calorie deficit is the holy trifecta that ultimately will lead to the success on your weight-loss

journey. In order to figure out your calorie deficit, you will need to calculate your maintenance calories, which is the number of calories you can eat in a day and still stay at the same weight. I used a TDEE (Total Daily Energy Expenditure) calculator that I found online to calculate my maintenance calories, and from there, I subtracted 10% to 20% from my maintenance calories to figure out what my deficit should be. For example, if my maintenance calories are 2,500, and I subtracted 10%, that would give me a deficit of 250 calories (2,500–250=2,250). Hypothetically, 2,250 calories is the maximum amount of calories I could eat in a day and still lose weight. The higher your deficit, the more weight you will lose. That being said, being extreme with calorie restriction and not eating healthy enough is not safe or sustainable and will only hurt your weight-loss efforts in the long run. A 10% to 15% caloric deficit is suitable for individuals aiming for slow and steady weight loss. This is a more conservative approach, reducing the risk of muscle loss and nutritional deficiencies. A 15% to 20% deficit is recommended for most people. It strikes a balance between effective weight loss and maintaining muscle mass and overall health.

It's essential to personalize the deficit based on individual factors such as current weight, metabolic health, activity level, and dietary preferences. Consulting with a healthcare professional or a dietitian is advisable in order to tailor a calorie deficit plan that fits your specific needs and goals. Not eating enough will deprive you of essential nutrients that your body needs, which can then lead to binging episodes and can actually slow down your metabolism, which in turn can slow down weight loss. The main goal of any diet should be achieving better health, not just losing weight.

Stay Active

Incorporating regular physical activity and workouts into your daily routine can significantly impact your results. Staying active contributes to weight loss by boosting metabolism, burning calories, and preserving lean body mass. Engaging in physical activities like cardio, strength training, and high-intensity interval training increases the body's energy expenditure, both during and after exercise. The increased metabolic rate helps burn more calories throughout the day, making it easier to create the calorie deficit necessary for weight loss. In addition, it's important to note that the goal of a healthy diet is fat loss, not muscle loss. Exercise plays a vital role in preserving lean muscle mass while losing fat. When people lose weight purely through diet alone, they tend to lose both muscle and fat. Incorporating strength training into your routine helps maintain lean muscle mass, which is crucial for a healthy metabolism and functional strength. Muscle tissue burns more calories at rest in comparison to fat tissue, further

aiding in weight loss and preventing the common pitfall of regaining weight once the diet ends. Starting a new exercise routine for weight loss is an exciting step toward better health, but it is crucial to approach this new endeavor with a mindset of progression. Taking it easy when beginning a workout regimen is not only beneficial for physical safety but also for long-term success and motivation. Set realistic goals for yourself and with time and practice, gradually increase the complexity of your workouts. This method will allow you to experience a sense of accomplishment and give you the motivation to continue all while aiding your weight loss. By easing into a new routine, you can build a strong foundation, prevent injuries, and maintain motivation, ultimately leading to more effective and sustainable weight loss.

Plan Meals Ahead

Planning meals ahead of time can be a very beneficial strategy for achieving weight-loss goals—it offers a range of benefits that will help you maintain a healthy diet, control portion sizes, and avoid the pitfalls of impulsive eating. One of the most common ways that people get off track with eating healthy is when they find themselves hungry, but they don't have healthy meals readily accessible to them. Taking the time to figure out what meals you want to cook for the week and shopping for these ingredients ahead of time is an important step in staying on track. Once you've figured out what meals you want to cook for the week, make a grocery list. This will save you time by knowing exactly what you're looking for in the grocery store and eliminate time aimlessly wandering through aisles. Having a list when grocery shopping will also ensure you have everything you need on hand to make your meals. When you do not have meals planned or healthy food readily available to you, it can be very easy to resort to eating fast food, snacks, or other convenience foods that are loaded with calories, refined sugars, and unhealthy fats. Planning your meals ahead of time helps you manage your time better and reduce stress; knowing what you are going to cook and eat in advance eliminates the daily scramble of deciding what to cook. A little planning will allow for a more structured day, which provides more time for other activities, like exercise. It also helps maintain consistency with eating healthy, which undoubtedly is the one of the keys to success when it comes to losing weight.

Use Meal Prep

I've included recipes in this book that can easily be prepared ahead of time so that you have delicious meals readily available throughout your weight-loss journey. Things like salad dressings are great to prep ahead of time to make your life easier when you're throwing together a salad.

STOCKING YOUR FRIDGE AND PANTRY

Stocking your fridge and pantry with essential items is the foundation of a well-equipped kitchen and will set you up for success. From staples that form the bases of many recipes to versatile ingredients that add flavor and nutrition, here is a curated list to ensure you are prepared for your culinary adventure. With these items on hand, you'll be ready to whip up delicious meals that will help you on your weight-loss journey.

- **GREEK YOGURT:** This is such a versatile ingredient to keep on hand; you can use it to make mains, desserts, and dressings. When paired with the right ingredients, Greek yogurt can make any recipe lighter in calories while also adding protein. Look for Greek yogurt options that are plain, unflavored, and contain 0% to 5% milk fat.

- **LOW-FAT COTTAGE CHEESE:** Low-fat cottage cheese is another ingredient that is very versatile and can be used in both sweet and savory dishes. It is a great low-calorie, high-protein substitute for higher-calorie ingredients like cream cheese, sour cream, milk, or heavy cream. Look for cottage cheese options that contain 0% to 4% milk fat.

- **REDUCED-FAT CHEESES:** Reduced-fat cheeses contain fewer calories, have a lower fat content than their full-fat counterparts, and can be used in the same way as regular cheeses in a variety of dishes. Look for options that are labeled "fat-free" or list reduced-fat percentages like 2% milk fat, on the packaging.

Commonly Used Spices and Condiments

Keeping these spices and condiments on hand will ensure you always have what you need to make many of the recipes in this book.

- Chicken bouillon granules
- Dried oregano
- Garlic powder
- Ground cumin
- Hot sauce
- Low-sodium taco seasoning
- Mustard (prepared and Dijon)
- Onion powder
- Paprika
- Sugar-free BBQ sauce
- Sugar-free ketchup

- **LOW-FAT MILKS:** Low-fat milks can be used in a wide range of recipes—from baking and cooking to smoothies and coffee. They function similarly to whole milk in most culinary applications, making them a versatile kitchen staple.

- **LOWER-CALORIE BREADS:** Lower-calorie bread options, like buns, flatbreads, and bagels, allow more flexibility in portion sizes, enabling you to enjoy bread as part of your balanced meal without exceeding your daily caloric limits. Look for breads that are labeled "light" or "low carb," or have the calories listed on the front of the packages. Some brands I like include Old Tyme 647 bread and buns, Sara Lee Delightful bread, and Franz Bakery Keto white bread and buns.

- **LOWER-CALORIE TORTILLAS AND WRAPS:** Tortillas and wraps are easy to store and have relatively long shelf lives, making them convenient and versatile options to have on hand. Look for options that are labeled "low carb" or "light." Some products I like include Mission Yellow Corn Tortillas, Mission Carb Balance Flour Tortillas, and La Banderita Carb Counter Flour Tortillas.

- **OLIVE OIL:** Olive oil can be used for sautéing, roasting, grilling, baking, and making salad dressings and marinades. Regular olive oil has a relatively high smoke point; its stability at high temperatures helps maintain its nutritional integrity during cooking, so it's better for cooking. Extra-virgin olive oil has a lower smoke point and is less ideal for high-temperature cooking, but its richer flavor makes it ideal for use in marinades and dressings.

- **OLIVE OIL COOKING SPRAY:** Cooking spray is great to keep on hand because it allows you to lightly coat food, pans, skillets, and baking dishes without using too much oil, which can help keep the calories and fat content lower.

- **FROZEN VEGETABLES:** Frozen vegetables provide a convenient, nutritious, and cost-effective option for incorporating more vegetables into your diet—plus they simplify meal planning and preparation. They cook quickly, making them ideal for those busy days when you don't have a lot of time to make dinner.

- **LEAFY GREENS:** Leafy greens like lettuce and salad spring mix are great for quickly throwing together meal salads or side salads. Both are nutritious and low in calories, which makes them great healthy eating options.

Natural Low-Calorie Sweeteners

Keeping low-calorie sweeteners, like stevia, erythritol, and monkfruit sugar on hand can be extremely beneficial because they provide the sweetness of sugar without the high calorie content, helping reduce your overall calorie intake.

- **STEVIA** is derived from the leaves of the *Stevia rebaudiana* plant, which is native to South America. The sweet compounds in stevia leaves are extracted and refined to produce a powdered or liquid sweetener. Stevia is much sweeter than sugar and is virtually calorie-free, making it a great option to reduce calorie intake or to manage blood sugar levels.

- **MONKFRUIT** is a small green gourd native to southern China. The sweet compounds in monkfruit are extracted to make a powdered or liquid sweetener. Like stevia, monkfruit is also much sweeter than sugar and virtually calorie-free.

- **ERYTHRITOL** is a sugar alcohol that occurs naturally in some fruits and fermented foods. It is typically produced by fermenting glucose from cornstarch or other plant sources. It is low in calories and does not metabolize in the same way as sugar, so its impact on blood sugar and insulin levels are minimal.

- **HONEY** is a natural sweetener with a distinct flavor that can really enhance recipes. It can be used as an alternative to refined sugar, offering a more wholesome sweetening option.

KITCHEN EQUIPMENT

Having the right equipment is essential for efficient cooking. The following list provides a small introduction to some of the key pieces of kitchen equipment that will help you tackle a wide range of recipes and culinary tasks.

- **AIR FRYER:** An air fryer provides speed and efficiency for cooking. In addition, it requires significantly less oil than traditional frying methods, resulting in foods that are lower in fat and calories. I recommend getting a medium- to large-size multifunction air fryer that offers the ability to adjust the cooking temperature and time, and has the capability to bake, roast, grill, and dehydrate.

- **BAKING SHEETS AND BAKING DISHES:** Baking sheets and dishes are essential for cooking foods in the oven. They are made to withstand the high temperatures of ovens and are handy for making healthy baked meals and desserts. I recommend getting baking sheets in sizes 9×13 inches (23×33cm), 10×15 inches (25.5×38cm), and 12×16 inches (30.5×40.5cm), and a baking dish that is 9×13 inches (23×33cm).

- **BLENDER:** A basic blender is a must for any kitchen. It's a versatile tool that allows you to prep a wide range of foods, including beverages, smoothies, soups, sauces, dips, and dressings. Blenders can quickly and easily mix ingredients, saving time in comparison to manual preparation methods.

- **BOX GRATER:** A box grater is a useful tool for all kinds of cooking tasks, from shredding vegetables to shredding fresh cheese.

- **COLANDERS AND STRAINERS:** Colanders and strainers are useful tools that help you wash and drain cooked pasta, rice, and vegetables, ensuring they are properly prepared for serving. They come in various sizes and mesh types, making them useful for sifting dry ingredients, straining sauces and soups, or separating solids from liquids.

- **KITCHEN SHEARS:** Kitchen shears are a highly versatile and useful tool that can help you cut meat, poultry, and vegetables. Kitchen shears also provide more control than a knife for certain tasks, reducing the risk of accidents. Shears can be handy to trim off fat or cut through poultry bones and joints, cutting up vegetables, or opening packages.

- **KNIVES AND CUTTING BOARDS:** Having sharp, high-quality knives on hand will make ingredient preparation quicker and more efficient, allowing you to slice, dice, chop, and mince ingredients with ease. High-quality cutting boards are complementary tools to the knives that will allow you to prepare food with more precision and safety. I recommend having a chef's knife, which is an all-purpose knife that's usually about 8 to 10 inches (20 to 35.5cm) in length and is used for chopping, slicing, dicing, and mincing. A paring knife is ideal for peeling and trimming. A serrated knife is great for cutting through bread and tomatoes.

- **MEASURING CUPS:** Measuring cups ensure that the ingredients you are using are the exact measurements that the recipe calls for, ensuring consistency in flavor and texture. Keep a set of dry measuring cups on hand, as well as a set of liquid measuring cups.

- **MEASURING SPOONS:** Measuring spoons provide precise measurements of small quantities of ingredients, which is crucial for ensuring proper flavor and texture.

- **MEAT THERMOMETER:** A meat thermometer ensures that meat and poultry are cooked to safe internal temperatures, reducing the risk of foodborne illnesses caused by consuming undercooked meats.

- **MIXING BOWLS:** Mixing bowls are great to have on hand because they make food preparation more efficient and convenient. They can be used to mix ingredients like salads and batters.

- **NONSTICK POTS AND PANS:** Nonstick pans can help reduce the amount of oil you use when you're cooking, which helps reduce both the fat and calorie contents of meals. They are designed to be long lasting and easy to clean due to their nonstick surfaces. I recommend pans with ceramic coatings, which typically are free of harmful chemicals. Try to stay away from Teflon-coated pans and pans coated with PFAS (per- and polyfluoroalkyl substances).

- **SLOW COOKER:** A slow cooker allows you to prepare a wide variety of meals including soups, stews, casseroles, and roasts, just to name a few. It promotes healthy cooking methods by minimizing the need for added fats and oil.

TIPS FOR STAYING ON TRACK

Staying on track with weight loss can be challenging, especially at the beginning of your journey when you're making big changes. You might not be accustomed to eating healthy meals all the time or working out regularly. The truth is, embarking on a weight-loss journey and staying on track will take effort on your behalf every single day. Here are some tips that can help you accomplish your weight-loss goals.

- **SET REALISTIC GOALS:** Start with setting small, achievable goals rather than making lots of drastic changes all at once. This will make it easier to stick to your plan, and you'll still feel a sense of accomplishment. Approach your plan as a day-by-day or even week-by-week plan rather than a month-by-month journey.

- **PLAN AND PREPARE YOUR MEALS:** Planning meals and snacks in advance can help you avoid impulsive eating and making unhealthy choices.

- **KEEP HEALTHY SNACKS ON HAND:** Having healthy snacks readily available will help curb hunger between meals, empowering you to continue your journey without falling to the temptation of high-calorie snacking. Some healthy snack options might include zero-sugar gelatin dessert, lower-calorie popcorn, zero-sugar pudding, fruits, nuts, and low-sugar yogurts.

- **FIND BALANCE:** Being too strict can be detrimental to a weight-loss journey. That feeling of extreme restriction can eventually lead you to falling off track. It's important to allow yourself occasional treats to avoid feeling deprived. Moderation is key; it's okay to occasionally indulge in your favorite foods in controlled portions.

- **TRACK YOUR PROGRESS:** Keep a food diary or use an app to track what you eat. This can help you stay accountable and identify patterns or triggers that can lead to overeating or undereating.

- **FOCUS ON PROTEIN INTAKE:** Getting sufficient protein with your meals is important because protein is the most filling macronutrient. Eating protein-rich foods will help you feel full longer, reducing your overall calorie intake and helping to control hunger and cravings. Additionally, adequate protein intake will help preserve lean muscle mass, which will help you lose fat instead of muscle.

- **AVOID TRIGGERS:** It's important to recognize and identify triggers that cause you to overeat. Some people eat out of boredom or stress. Exercise can reduce stress and improve your mood, making you less likely to turn to food for comfort. Engaging in hobbies you enjoy, such as reading, gardening, or painting, can help distract you from emotional eating. This is where keeping healthy snacks on hand and avoiding keeping unhealthy foods at home can be very beneficial. Understanding your triggers and implementing strategies for dealing with them can help you develop healthier habits that will aid in weight loss.

- **BE SMART WHEN DINING OUT:** Dining out while on a weight-loss journey can be challenging, as most foods are high in calories and fat, which can easily put you out of a calorie deficit. Before you go out, I recommend planning ahead, looking at the restaurant's menu online, and deciding on a healthy option ahead of arriving at the restaurant. Many restaurants provide nutritional information that can help you make informed choices. Eat a light, healthy snack before going out to avoid arriving at the restaurant overly hungry, which can lead to overeating. Prioritize lean protein and vegetables when eating, and try to avoid fried foods.

- **DRINK SMART:** Avoid sugary drinks and alcoholic beverages, which can add unnecessary calories. Try to stick to water, sparkling water, or unsweetened drinks. Avoiding high-calorie drinks is an effective strategy for weight loss, as beverages can contribute a significant number of hidden calories.

- **FORGIVE YOURSELF:** If you slip up, don't be too hard on yourself. Recognize that setbacks are normal and then focus on getting back on track rather than dwelling on the occasional slip-up.

Implementing these tips can help create a sustainable approach to dieting and make it easier to maintain healthy eating habits in the long term.

" IT'S OKAY TO OCCASIONALLY INDULGE IN YOUR FAVORITE FOODS IN CONTROLLED PORTIONS

BREA

FAST

TROPICAL COCONUT CHIA SEED PUDDING

PREP TIME: 7 minutes plus overnight

COOK TIME: none

MAKES: 3 servings

SERVING SIZE: 1½ cups

9 tbsp chia seeds

2 (13.5fl oz/400ml) cans reduced-fat coconut milk

3 tsp vanilla extract

4 packets stevia (about 1 heaping tbsp)

1 large fresh mango, diced

2 tbsp shredded coconut (optional)

I love this indulgent and creamy breakfast dish because I love anything coconut, so you can imagine the relief I felt when I found that reduced-fat coconut milk does actually exist! Topping this pudding with mango and shredded coconut really elevates it by adding a touch of sweetness.

1. Add the chia seeds, coconut milk, vanilla extract, and stevia to a large bowl. Stir to combine, cover tightly, and then place in the fridge to thicken overnight.

2. When ready to serve, divide the pudding into three separate containers. Top each serving with equal amounts of diced mango and shredded coconut.

3. Store any leftovers in an airtight container in the fridge for up to 4 days.

Nutrition (per serving):

CALORIES: 297

TOTAL FAT: 20g

TOTAL CARBOHYDRATE: 21g

PROTEIN: 8g

NOTE: For the sweetener, I usually add 2 to 3 packets of stevia, but you can also substitute 3 to 4 tablespoons of honey if you prefer not to use stevia. Adjust the amount of sweetener to your liking.

STRAWBERRY-BANANA OVERNIGHT OATS

PREP TIME: 10 minutes plus overnight

COOK TIME: none

MAKES: 1 serving

SERVING SIZE: 1 cup

½ cup rolled oats

1 tbsp chia seeds

6 large fresh strawberries

1 large ripe banana

1 cup unsweetened plain almond milk (or milk of your choice)

1 tbsp vanilla extract

1 tbsp honey, plus extra to taste

Pinch of salt

Sliced strawberries, for topping (optional)

One of my favorite breakfasts on my weight-loss journey has been these overnight oats. They're super easy to make, quick to assemble, and they contain a combination of complex carbohydrates, protein, fiber, and healthy fats that will help keep you feeling full and energized.

1. Combine the rolled oats and chia seeds in a resealable container. Set aside.

2. Add the strawberries, banana, almond milk, vanilla extract, honey, and salt to a blender. Blend until smooth.

3. Add the strawberry-banana mixture to the oat and chia seed mixture. Mix well.

4. Cover the container and refrigerate for at least 4 hours or overnight.

5. Stir the oats before eating and top with sliced strawberries (if using).

Nutrition (per serving):

CALORIES: 413

TOTAL FAT: 10g

TOTAL CARBOHYDRATE: 70g

PROTEIN: 10g

NOTE: I like to triple this recipe and meal prep 3 containers of these oats for quick grab-and-go snacks or breakfasts on busy days.

RED VELVET OATMEAL PANCAKES

PREP TIME: 5 minutes

COOK TIME: 10 minutes

MAKES: 4 pancakes

SERVING SIZE: 4 pancakes

1 medium banana

½ cup rolled oats

1 large egg

¼ cup unsweetened almond milk

1 tsp vanilla extract

1 tsp baking powder

1 tbsp unsweetened cacao powder

1 tsp red food coloring

Pinch of salt

Olive oil cooking spray

¼ cup nonfat vanilla Greek yogurt (optional)

½ cup sliced fresh strawberries (optional)

Low-sugar pancake syrup of your choice

These oatmeal pancakes are my go-to whenever I'm craving pancakes because they are so much healthier than their flour counterparts. The oatmeal makes them high in fiber, which can help regulate digestion, lower cholesterol levels, and keep you feeling full longer.

1. In a blender, combine the banana, oats, egg, almond milk, vanilla extract, baking powder, cacao powder, red food coloring, and salt. Blend until smooth.

2. Spray a large skillet with olive oil cooking spray and preheat over medium heat.

3. Once the skillet is hot, pour enough batter into the pan to make 1 pancake. Cook the pancake until it starts to bubble, about 2 to 3 minutes, then flip and cook for another 2 to 3 minutes or until golden brown. Repeat with the remaining batter.

4. Top with vanilla Greek yogurt (if using) and strawberries (if using), then drizzle the syrup over the top.

Nutrition (per serving):

CALORIES: 415

TOTAL FAT: 8g

TOTAL CARBOHYDRATE: 61g

PROTEIN: 13g

HIGH-PROTEIN EGG WHITE OMELET

PREP TIME: 5 minutes

COOK TIME: 10 minutes

MAKES: 1 omelet

SERVING SIZE: 1 omelet

3 egg whites
1 large egg
½ tsp salt
½ tsp black pepper
1 cup fresh baby spinach
2oz (57g) turkey ham, chopped
Olive oil cooking spray
¼ cup crumbled fat-free feta
Chopped fresh chives (optional)

When you think of good weight-loss breakfasts, egg white omelets are one of the first things that come to mind. I make egg white omelets frequently because they're filling but still on the lower calorie side. This omelet is fluffy, light, and packed full of protein. The tanginess of the feta compliments the savory turkey ham, while the spinach adds a pop of color and freshness.

1. Add the egg whites, egg, salt, and pepper to a medium bowl. Whisk to combine.

2. Lightly spray a 7-inch (18cm) skillet with olive oil cooking spray. Preheat the skillet over medium heat. Add the baby spinach and cook until wilted, about 1 to 2 minutes. Add the egg mixture and then place the turkey ham on top. Reduce the heat to medium-low, cover, and cook for 3 to 5 minutes.

3. Once the top of the omelet is almost cooked, sprinkle the feta over the turkey ham and then fold the omelet in half. Continue cooking for 2 to 4 minutes more or until completely cooked. If desired, top with a sprinkle of chopped fresh chives.

Nutrition (per serving):

CALORIES: 230
TOTAL FAT: 5g
TOTAL CARBOHYDRATE: 6g
PROTEIN: 36g

"MY PANTS ARE FALLING OFF" BREAKFAST BOWL

PREP TIME: 10 minutes

COOK TIME: 20 minutes

MAKES: 1 bowl

SERVING SIZE: 1 bowl

2 tsp olive oil, divided

1 medium yellow potato, peeled and diced

4oz (113g) ground turkey sausage

1 large egg

¼ cup fat-free shredded cheddar cheese

3 tbsp **Jalapeño-Lime Ranch Dressing** (p. 92) (optional)

For the pico de gallo:

1 Roma tomato, diced

¼ medium white onion, diced

2 tbsp chopped cilantro leaves

¼ tsp salt

¼ tsp black pepper

½ tsp garlic powder

Juice of ½ lime

For the guacamole:

½ medium avocado, diced

½ tsp cumin

Juice of ½ lime

Salt, to taste

Black pepper, to taste

Garlic powder, to taste

I'm a big fan of bowls, and enjoying a bowl for breakfast is no exception. This flavorful breakfast has everything you need to fuel your morning, from carbs to protein and healthy fats. Using leaner meat like turkey sausage really makes a difference in keeping this hearty breakfast bowl on the lighter side.

1. To make the pico de gallo, combine the tomatoes, onion, cilantro, salt, pepper, garlic powder, and lime juice in a large mixing bowl. Mix well and set aside.

2. To make the guacamole, place the avocado in a small bowl and mash until smooth. Add the cumin and lime juice, mix well, then season to taste with salt, pepper, and garlic powder.

3. Add 1 teaspoon of the olive oil to a large skillet over medium-low heat. When the oil is hot, add the potato and 2 tablespoons of water. Cover with a lid and cook for 10 minutes or until the potatoes are fork-tender, stirring every 2 to 3 minutes to brown the potatoes on all sides. Transfer the potatoes to a large bowl.

4. Crumble the sausage into the skillet. Place the skillet back over the heat and adjust the heat to medium. Cook until fully cooked through. Transfer the sausage to the bowl with the potatoes.

5. Heat the remaining 1 teaspoon of olive oil in the skillet. Add the egg and scramble until fully cooked.

6. Place the scrambled egg in the bowl with the potatoes and sausage. Top with the pico de gallo, guacamole, and cheddar cheese. If desired, spoon the Jalapeño-Lime Ranch Dressing over the top. Enjoy!

Nutrition (per serving):

CALORIES: 568

TOTAL FAT: 22g

TOTAL CARBOHYDRATE: 39g

PROTEIN: 39g

TORTILLA ESPAÑOLA

PREP TIME: 10 minutes

COOK TIME:
30 minutes

MAKES: 2 servings

SERVING SIZE:
½ tortilla

2 large yellow potatoes,
   washed, peeled, and diced
3 tsp olive oil, divided
1 tsp salt
½ cup diced yellow onion
4 large eggs
1 tsp garlic powder

A Spanish tortilla isn't actually a tortilla as we know it, but rather a potato omelet. It's a traditional Spanish dish I was introduced to by my father. Spaniards will eat this at any moment of the day, but it's been popularized as a breakfast dish. I grew up eating it and it is easily one of my favorite breakfast recipes. Traditionally, a Tortilla Española is fried in oil, making it a pretty high-calorie, high-fat dish, but this recipe minimizes the oil, resulting in a lower-calorie version of the delicious Spanish tortilla that I love so much.

1. Add the diced potatoes, 1 teaspoon of the olive oil, and salt to a microwave-safe bowl. Toss the potatoes to coat with oil, then cover the bowl with a plate and microwave for 3 minutes or until fork-tender.

2. Add 1 teaspoon of the olive oil to an 8-inch (20cm) skillet placed over medium heat. When the oil is hot, add the potatoes and onion. Brown for 5 to 7 minutes, stirring occasionally, then remove from the heat to cool for 5 minutes. Transfer the potatoes to a bowl and then wipe the skillet clean.

3. Add the eggs and garlic powder to a medium bowl. Whisk until combined, then add the potatoes. Stir.

4. Place the skillet back over medium heat. Add the remaining 1 teaspoon of olive oil. When the oil is hot, add the potato and egg mixture, and use a spatula to spread the mixture evenly. Cover the skillet and cook for 5 minutes or until the egg is just set and the tortilla is slightly puffed.

5. Carefully place a large plate over the top of the skillet and then flip the skillet to transfer the tortilla to the plate. Place the tortilla back in the skillet with the uncooked side down. Cook for 2 minutes more or until set. Cut into wedges to serve.

6. Store any leftovers in an airtight container in the fridge for up to 4 days.

Nutrition (per serving):

CALORIES: 313

TOTAL FAT: 16g

TOTAL CARBOHYDRATE: 26g

PROTEIN: 15g

NOTE: The potatoes are initially cooked in the microwave to reduce the amount of oil in the dish.

EGG AND TURKEY BACON QUESADILLA

PREP TIME: 5 minutes

COOK TIME: 10 minutes

MAKES: 1 quesadilla

SERVING SIZE: 1 quesadilla

Olive oil cooking spray

3 slices uncured turkey bacon, diced

¼ medium red onion, diced

½ medium green bell pepper, diced

½ Roma tomato, diced

½ tsp Cajun seasoning

½ tsp black pepper

1 large egg

2 egg whites

½ cup shredded reduced-fat cheddar cheese, divided

1 tortilla wrap (I use Mission Carb Balance wraps)

For the Lean & Mean Dipping Sauce:

½ cup light mayonnaise

1 tbsp sriracha

½ tsp garlic powder

⅛ tsp salt

This egg and turkey bacon quesadilla is high in protein, filling, and so easy to make. It's a flavorful way to get some healthy protein first thing in the morning. Using a mixture of egg, egg whites, reduced-fat cheese, and turkey bacon creates a lower-calorie quesadilla that is lighter but still delicious.

1. Make the Lean & Mean Dipping Sauce by combining the mayonnaise, sriracha, garlic powder, and salt in a small bowl. Stir until well combined. Set aside.

2. Lightly coat an 8-inch (20cm) skillet with olive oil cooking spray and place over medium heat. Add the turkey bacon slices to the skillet and fully cook. Once cooked, mince and set aside.

3. To the same skillet, add the onion, bell pepper, tomato, Cajun seasoning, and black pepper. Sauté until completely cooked through, then remove the veggies from the skillet and set aside.

4. Add the egg and egg whites to a medium bowl. Whisk to combine. Spray the skillet with additional olive oil cooking spray and then place the skillet back over medium heat. Add the eggs and scramble until cooked.

5. Wipe the skillet clean and place it back over medium heat. Place the tortilla in the skillet, then place ¼ cup of the cheese on one half of the tortilla. Place the scrambled eggs on top of the cheese, followed by the turkey bacon, veggies, and remaining ¼ cup of cheese. Fold the other half of the tortilla on top of the fillings and then cook for 5 minutes, flipping the quesadilla halfway through the cooking time to ensure both sides of the tortilla brown and the cheese is melted. Cut into wedges. Serve with the Lean & Mean Dipping Sauce on the side.

6. Store any leftovers in an airtight container in the fridge for up to 4 days.

Nutrition (per serving):

CALORIES: 401

TOTAL FAT: 18g

TOTAL CARBOHYDRATE: 26g

PROTEIN: 44g

BREAKFAST TOSTADAS

PREP TIME: 5 minutes
COOK TIME: 15 minutes
MAKES: 2 servings
SERVING SIZE: 1 tostada

2 tostadas
   (I use Guerrero brand)
2 large eggs
¼ tsp salt
¼ tsp black pepper
Olive oil cooking spray
½ cup fat-free refried beans,
   warmed and divided
½ medium avocado, sliced
Green salsa, for topping (I use
   Herdez Salsa Verde)
1 pickled jalapeño, sliced
   (optional)
Green onions, for topping
   (optional)
Diced tomatoes, for topping
   (optional)

Any time is a good time for a tostada, and breakfast is no exception. These delicious breakfast tostadas include many of the same traditional yet simple ingredients that I grew up eating, but these are made lighter by using lower-calorie corn tortillas. They offer a hearty and satisfying start to the day, combining savory flavors with the crunch of a tortilla.

---

1. Place the tortillas in an air fryer. Air-fry at 400°F (205°C) for about 10 minutes or until crispy. (If you don't have an air fryer, you can bake the tortillas at 375°F [190°C] for 8 to 10 minutes.)

2. Whisk the eggs, salt, and pepper together in a small bowl. Lightly spray a medium skillet with olive oil cooking spray and then place over medium heat. Add the eggs and scramble until just set.

3. Spread ¼ cup of the refried beans over a tostada. Place half the scrambled eggs on top, then top with half the sliced avocado and the desired amount of green salsa. If desired, top with half of the jalapeño slices, half of the green onions, and half of the tomatoes. Repeat with the remaining ingredients.

Nutrition (per serving):

CALORIES: 233
TOTAL FAT: 13g
TOTAL CARBOHYDRATE: 21g
PROTEIN: 9g

NOTE: I highly recommend topping these tostadas with a dollop of pico de gallo to really take them over the top!

RASPBERRY BREAKFAST PARFAIT

PREP TIME: 25 minutes
COOK TIME: none
MAKES: 1 parfait
SERVING SIZE: 1 parfait

1 cup fresh raspberries, plus extra for topping
2 tbsp chia seeds
1 tbsp honey
1 cup plain nonfat Greek yogurt, divided
½ cup granola, divided

This is a classic breakfast that is delicious and offers a nice boost of protein to kick-start your morning. I use a super-easy-to-make homemade raspberry jam that is high in fiber, low in sugar, and rich in nutrients from both the raspberry and chia seeds. The granola gives this parfait a beautiful crunch amongst the creaminess of the yogurt and jam.

1. Combine the raspberries, chia seeds, ¼ cup water, and honey in a medium bowl. Mash to create a jam-like consistency, then set the mixture aside to thicken for 20 minutes in the fridge.

2. To a 16-ounce jar, add ½ cup of the Greek yogurt, followed by half of the raspberry jam and then ¼ cup of the granola. Add the remaining ½ cup of Greek yogurt on top of the granola, followed by the remaining raspberry jam and remaining ¼ cup of granola.

3. If desired, top with extra raspberries and enjoy!

Nutrition (per serving):

CALORIES: 441
TOTAL FAT: 13g
TOTAL CARBOHYDRATE: 52g
PROTEIN: 31g

NOTE: This is a great meal prep recipe for a quick breakfast or as a snack on those busier days.

CLEAR-FACE-CARD GREEN JUICE

PREP TIME: 5 minutes
COOK TIME: none
MAKES: 4 cups
SERVING SIZE: 1 cup

5 medium Granny Smith
  apples, sliced, with cores
  and seeds removed
1 medium cucumber, peeled
3 tbsp aloe vera juice
Small bunch fresh cilantro
Juice of 1 lime

What you put in your body is often reflected in your skin. Once I began eating healthier and prioritizing green juices over diet sodas, I noticed a huge difference in my skin. Green juices help your body get the nutrients it needs.

1. Add all the ingredients to a juicer. Process to extract all the juice from the pulp.

2. Pour into a glass and enjoy. Store in the fridge for up to 3 days or freeze and thaw when ready to drink.

Nutrition (per serving):

CALORIES: 95
TOTAL FAT: 0g
TOTAL CARBOHYDRATE: 25g
PROTEIN: 1g

NOTES: If you don't like cilantro, feel free to replace it with parsley. I usually make enough of this green juice to last me a few days, and I'll drink one each day. If you don't have a juicer, you can use a blender. Add 3 cups of water to the blender and strain the pulp from the juice.

WILD BLUEBERRY SMOOTHIE

PREP TIME: 5 minutes

COOK TIME: none

MAKES: 3 servings

SERVING SIZE: 1 cup

1 cup baby spinach

1 cup frozen wild blueberries

1 large banana, peeled and frozen

1 tbsp honey

½ medium avocado

1 tbsp flax seed

1 tbsp almond butter

2 cups unsweetened almond milk

I love anything that has wild blueberries in it, and this anti-inflammatory smoothie is no exception. Not only does it taste heavenly, but it also has so many nutritional benefits, including antioxidants from the blueberries, as well as fiber and healthy fats from other ingredients.

1. Combine all the ingredients in a blender. Blend until smooth.

2. Pour into glass. Enjoy!

Nutrition (per serving):

CALORIES: 219

TOTAL FAT: 10g

TOTAL CARBOHYDRATE: 30g

PROTEIN: 4g

NOTE: If desired, top with a few extra flax seeds for added nutrition benefits and texture. You can also add a serving of your favorite unflavored protein powder to make this a delicious protein drink.

MAKE-ME-GLOW JUICE

PREP TIME: 5 minutes
COOK TIME: none
MAKES: 1 serving
SERVING SIZE:
16fl oz (473ml)

4 large carrots, peeled
1 large cucumber, peeled
1 large Honeycrisp apple, sliced, cores and seeds removed
1 large lemon
1 large orange
1 knob fresh ginger
1 tbsp turmeric powder
1 tbsp black pepper

This juice has all the ingredients to help aid glowy skin, reduce inflammation, and improve digestion. The combination of black pepper and turmeric is powerful; they magnify each other's effects leading to greater health benefits for you.

1. Add all the ingredients to a juicer. Process to extract all the juice from the pulp.
2. Pour into a glass and enjoy.

Nutrition (per serving):

CALORIES: 105
TOTAL FAT: 0g
TOTAL CARBOHYDRATE: 25g
PROTEIN: 2g

NOTE: If you do not own a juicer, remove the citrus skins, blend all the ingredients in a blender, then strain out the pulp.

CHOCOLATE PROTEIN SMOOTHIE

PREP TIME: 5 minutes

COOK TIME: none

MAKES: 1 serving

SERVING SIZE: 2 cups

1 medium frozen banana

1 scoop chocolate protein powder

¼ tsp ground cinnamon

1 tbsp flax seeds

1 tbsp unsweetened cacao powder

I'm a chocolate lover and this smoothie does not disappoint. In addition to the protein, this smoothie is a great source of healthy fats from the flax seeds, and vitamins and minerals from the banana. This is one of my favorite ways to hit my protein goal for those days when I need an extra boost.

1. Combine all the ingredients and 1½ cups water in a blender. Blend until smooth.

2. Pour into a glass and enjoy!

Nutrition (per serving):

CALORIES: 281

TOTAL FAT: 5g

TOTAL CARBOHYDRATE: 38g

PROTEIN: 25g

NOTES: Be sure to peel the banana before freezing it. The amount of protein in this smoothie will vary depending on the protein powder you use.

IMMUNE-TO-MY-HATERS SHOTS

PREP TIME: 10 minutes

COOK TIME: none

MAKES: about 10 shots

SERVING SIZE:
1 (2fl oz/60ml) shot

2 medium lemons, peeled
1 medium orange, peeled
½ lb (226g) fresh ginger
1 tbsp turmeric powder
1 tsp black pepper
2 cups coconut water
   (if using a blender)

These shots are potent and made by blending immune-boosting ingredients. They have a strong and spicy flavor, so prepare for a kick! Ginger contains compounds like gingerols and shogaol, which have anti-inflammatory and antioxidant properties that may help strengthen the immune system. I like to enjoy one shot each day!

1. Add all the ingredients to a juicer and extract the juice from the pulp.

2. Pour the juice into a shot glass and enjoy.

3. Store any leftovers in an airtight container in the fridge for up to 3 days or freeze and thaw the shots when you're ready to drink them.

Nutrition (per serving):

CALORIES: 25
TOTAL FAT: 0g
TOTAL CARBOHYDRATE: 6g
PROTEIN: 0g

NOTE: If you don't have a juicer, you can use a blender. Add 2 cups of coconut water and strain the pulp from the juice.

LUNCH

SHRIMP SPRING ROLLS

PREP TIME: 10 minutes

COOK TIME:
10 minutes

MAKES: 6 rolls

SERVING SIZE: 2 rolls

1 head baby romaine lettuce

1 shallot, peeled and chopped

3 garlic cloves, chopped

1 lb (454g) raw jumbo shrimp, peeled and deveined

6 rice-paper wrappers

¼ medium red cabbage, shredded

1 large cucumber, julienned

2 medium carrots, julienned

1 medium red bell pepper, julienned

1 small bunch fresh mint leaves, torn

For the peanut sauce:

2 tbsp creamy peanut butter

2 tbsp low-sodium soy sauce

1 tbsp rice vinegar

2 tbsp honey

1 garlic clove, minced

Nutrition (per serving):

CALORIES: 350

TOTAL FAT: 3g

TOTAL CARBOHYDRATE: 40g

PROTEIN: 35g

NOTE: Be careful not to soak the wrappers in the water for too long, as they can become very soft and tear when you're assembling the rolls.

These shrimp spring rolls are a light and refreshing Vietnamese snack and are made by wrapping cooked shrimp, fresh vegetables, and mint in a rice-paper wrapper. Spring rolls offer a delightful combination of flavors and textures that provide a taste of freshness in each bite. The peanut sauce brings it all together to make this an amazing lunch.

1. Make the peanut sauce by combining the peanut butter, soy sauce, rice vinegar, honey, and garlic in a small bowl. Mix to combine. Set aside.

2. Pull 6 romaine lettuce leaves from the stem. Wash and dry the leaves, then cut them so they will fit in the spring roll wrappers.

3. Fill a medium saucepan with water and place over high heat. Add the shallot and garlic cloves and then bring to a boil. Once boiling, add the shrimp, cover the pot with a lid, then remove from the heat. Poach the shrimp for 2 to 3 minutes, then use a slotted spoon to transfer the shrimp from the pot to an ice bath. Allow the shrimp to cool for 2 to 4 minutes, then remove them from the ice bath and set aside to drain on a paper towel.

4. Take 1 rice-paper wrapper and soak it in warm water for 3 to 5 seconds or until the wrapper just begins to soften. Lay the wrapper flat on a clean surface. Begin assembling the rolls by placing a lettuce leaf toward the bottom of the wrapper and then topping the leaf with pinches of red cabbage, cucumber, carrots, red pepper, and mint leaves.

5. Place 3 to 4 shrimp next to the veggies and then begin rolling the wrapper from the bottom as you tuck the veggies into the wrapper. Fold the uncovered sides inward and then tightly roll the wrapper up the rest of the way. Repeat the process until all 6 spring rolls are done. Enjoy with the peanut sauce served on the side for dipping.

CHICKEN-AVOCADO LETTUCE CUPS

PREP TIME: 10 minutes

COOK TIME: none

MAKES: 6 boats

SERVING SIZE: 3 boats

1 head Bibb lettuce

2 large Haas avocados

2 skinless rotisserie chicken breasts, chopped

Juice of 1 lime

½ cup fresh cilantro, chopped

½ large red onion, diced

1 tbsp garlic powder, plus more to taste

1 tsp salt, plus more to taste

1 tsp black pepper, plus more to taste

Think of this recipe almost as a marriage between guacamole and chicken salad, but without the mayo! These boats are a light, flavorful high-protein meal that will leave you feeling satisfied. The healthy fat and creaminess from the avocado complement the brightness of the cilantro and lime in every bite.

1. Tear off 6 lettuce leaves to create the "cups." Rinse and dry the leaves.

2. Add the avocados to a large bowl and mash until smooth. Add the chicken, lime juice, cilantro, onion, garlic powder, salt, and pepper. Mix well to combine, then taste and add additional garlic powder, salt, and pepper, if desired.

3. Spoon ½ cup of the chicken salad into a lettuce cup. Repeat with the remaining ingredients.

4. Store any leftovers in an airtight container in the fridge for up to 4 days.

Nutrition (per serving):

CALORIES: 481

TOTAL FAT: 25g

TOTAL CARBOHYDRATE: 15g

PROTEIN: 50g

REVENGE BODY PIZZA

PREP TIME: 5 minutes

COOK TIME: 10 minutes

MAKES: 1 pizza

SERVING SIZE: 1 pizza

1 (9×12-inch/23×30cm) lavash bread

Olive oil cooking spray

¼ cup low-sodium pizza sauce

½ cup reduced-fat shredded mozzarella, divided

17 slices (30g) turkey pepperoni

¼ tsp dried oregano, for topping

¼ tsp garlic powder, for topping

½ tsp crushed red pepper flakes, for topping

Fresh arugula, to serve (optional)

Who doesn't love pizza?! I know I do! However, when you're trying to stay on a calorie deficit, eating a slice of high-calorie pizza can really take up a lot of your calories for a day or even put you over your deficit. This flatbread pizza will kick your pizza craving and leave you feeling full.

1. Preheat the oven to 400°F (205°C). Lightly spray the lavash bread with olive oil cooking spray on both sides and then toast for 3 to 5 minutes or until golden. Remove the toasted lavash bread from the oven and reduce the oven temperature to 350°F (175°C).

2. Spread the pizza sauce over the bread. Top with half the shredded mozzarella, add the turkey pepperoni, then sprinkle the remaining mozzarella over the top.

3. Place the pizza in the oven and bake for 3 minutes or until the cheese is melted.

4. Season with the oregano, garlic powder, and chili flakes, then top with fresh arugula (if using). Eat the entire pizza guilt-free!

Nutrition (per serving):

CALORIES: 365

TOTAL FAT: 17g

TOTAL CARBOHYDRATE: 21g

PROTEIN: 38g

NOTE: Be careful not to burn the pizza when baking the bread the second time. Since the lavash bread is so thin, it can easily burn, so keep a very close eye on it.

SALMON CUCUMBER BOATS

PREP TIME: 15 minutes

COOK TIME: 20 minutes

MAKES: 1 servings

SERVING SIZE: 2 boats

1 (5oz/142g) skinless salmon fillet, diced

1 tsp garlic powder

1 tsp onion powder

½ tsp salt

1 tsp black pepper

1 tsp paprika

Olive oil cooking spray

1 large cucumber, washed and dried

½ cup uncooked jasmine rice

1 cup water

Furikake (Japanese rice seasoning), for topping

2 tbsp chopped green onion

For the Spicy Sriracha Sauce:

¼ cup plain nonfat Greek yogurt

1 tbsp sriracha

1 tbsp honey

These boats are light, refreshing, and will help keep you satisfied while you're in a calorie deficit. The crisp and cool cucumber offers a refreshing base that contrasts nicely with the rich and savory flavor of the salmon.

1. Make the Spicy Sriracha Sauce by combining the Greek yogurt, sriracha, and honey in a small bowl. Mix well to combine. Add 1 to 2 tablespoons of water, 1 tablespoon at a time, until the sauce reaches a pourable consistency. Set aside.

2. Combine the salmon, garlic powder, onion powder, salt, pepper, and paprika in a small bowl. Toss to coat the salmon in the seasonings. Lightly spray a large skillet with olive oil cooking spray and place over medium heat. Add the salmon and cook for 3 to 5 minutes or until fully cooked through.

3. Place the rice in a mesh strainer and rinse under cold water until the water runs clear.

4. Add 1 cup of water to a medium pot and bring to a boil over high heat. Add the rice, stir, then reduce the heat to low. Cover and allow to simmer for 15 to 20 minutes or until the water is absorbed and the rice is tender. Remove from the heat and allow to sit, covered, for 5 to 10 minutes more to allow the rice to continue to steam. Gently fluff the rice with a fork, separating any grains that may be stuck together.

5. Slice the ends off the cucumber and then slice the cucumber in half vertically. Scoop out the seeds and enough flesh that the cucumber halves are hollowed out, leaving some flesh intact.

6. Assemble the boats by filling each cucumber half with 3 to 4 tablespoons of cooked rice, the salmon, a sprinkling of furikake, a drizzle of the Spicy Sriracha Sauce, and a sprinkle of green onions.

Nutrition (per serving):

CALORIES: 424

TOTAL FAT: 12g

TOTAL CARBOHYDRATE: 33g

PROTEIN: 33g

PIZZA BURRITOS

PREP TIME: 10 minutes

COOK TIME: 15 minutes

MAKES: 2 burritos

SERVING SIZE: 1 burrito

1 tbsp olive oil

½ medium white onion, sliced

½ cup ground Italian turkey sausage

Pinch of salt

Pinch of black pepper

2 lower-calorie burrito wraps (I use Mission Carb Balance Burrito-Size Tortillas)

6 tbsp no-sugar-added marinara sauce, divided (I use Primal Kitchen Tomato-Basil Marinara)

20 slices turkey pepperoni, divided

½ cup shredded reduced-fat mozzarella, divided

¼ cup fresh basil, thinly sliced and divided

These burritos combine all the flavors of pizza in a burrito. To keep this lower in calories, I used turkey sausage, which is leaner than pork, as well as lower-calorie burrito wraps and lower-sugar marinara. I'm a huge advocate for still eating foods you enjoy by choosing healthier options, and this dish is the direct result of that philosophy.

1. Heat the olive oil in a medium skillet over medium heat. When the oil is hot, add the onion and turkey sausage and then season with the salt and pepper. Cook until the sausage is browned and the onion is soft, about 5 to 7 minutes, while using a wooden spoon to stir the ingredients occasionally and break up the sausage.

2. Place the burrito wraps on a flat surface. Divide the marinara sauce between the wraps and then add equal amounts of the sausage mixture, pepperoni, mozzarella, and basil to the center of each wrap. Roll the wraps into burritos.

3. Place the burritos, seam sides down, in a large skillet over medium heat. Heat for 2 to 3 minutes per side or until browned.

4. Store any leftovers in an airtight container in the fridge for up to 4 days.

Nutrition (per serving):

CALORIES: 309

TOTAL FAT: 19g

TOTAL CARBOHYDRATE: 38g

PROTEIN: 23g

LETTUCE-WRAPPED TURKEY BURGERS

PREP TIME: 10 minutes

COOK TIME: 15 minutes

MAKES: 4 servings

SERVINGS: 1 burger

2 tbsp olive oil, divided

1 medium white onion, sliced

1 lb (454g) 93%-lean ground turkey

½ cup panko breadcrumbs

2 tbsp Worcestershire sauce

1 large egg

1 tbsp garlic powder

1 tbsp onion powder

½ tsp salt

1 tsp black pepper

4 slices fat-free cheddar cheese

2 medium heads iceberg lettuce

4 slices beefsteak tomato

12 dill pickle slices

2 tbsp no-sugar-added ketchup

2 tbsp yellow mustard

These lettuce-wrapped turkey burgers are lower-calorie alternatives to traditional burgers. I love making these on those days when I want to eat a lighter meal. The crisp lettuce replaces the traditional burger bun and offers a refreshing bite. The burger patty is made from lean ground turkey to keep it light but it's still full of flavor.

---

1. Add 1 tablespoon of olive oil to a medium skillet over medium heat. When the oil is hot, add the onion slices and sauté until soft and lightly browned. Set aside.

2. Add the ground turkey, breadcrumbs, Worcestershire sauce, egg, garlic powder, onion powder, salt, and pepper to a large bowl. Mix well and then divide into 4 patties.

3. Add the remaining 1 tablespoon of olive oil to a medium skillet over medium heat. Fully cook the burger patties, then place a slice of cheddar on top of each burger. Cover the skillet with a lid and allow the cheese to melt for about 1 to 2 minutes.

4. Cut 1 head of lettuce in half widthwise. Remove the outermost leaves and most of the core from each half. Cut each half into two pieces to create the "buns." Repeat with the second head of lettuce.

5. Smear the bottom of one of the lettuce "buns" with 1 tablespoon ketchup and 1 tablespoon mustard, then place a turkey patty, 1 quarter of the onions, a tomato slice, and 3 pickle slices on top. Top with the half of the lettuce "bun." Repeat with the remaining burger ingredients to create 4 burgers.

6. Store any leftovers in an airtight container in the fridge for up to 4 days.

Nutrition (per serving):

CALORIES: 272

TOTAL FAT: 12g

TOTAL CARBOHYDRATE: 15g

PROTEIN: 26g

NOTES: Feel free to use the **Big Momma Burger Sauce** (p. 127) in place of the ketchup and mustard for this burger.

CRUNCHY BBQ CHICKEN WRAPS

PREP TIME: 10 minutes
COOK TIME: 5 minutes
MAKES: 4 servings
SERVING SIZE: 1 wrap

2½ cups shredded, cooked chicken breast

1 cup shredded reduced-fat cheddar cheese

¼ cup chopped fresh cilantro

¼ cup chopped red onion

½ cup sugar-free BBQ sauce

4 lower-calorie burrito-size flour tortillas

2 tbsp olive oil

2 cups shredded romaine lettuce, for topping (optional)

Low-fat sour cream, for topping (optional)

Hot sauce, for topping (optional)

These wraps are super simple to make and so full of flavor. The sugar-free BBQ sauce and lower-calorie tortillas help keep them healthy, but they still have that delicious sweet and smoky BBQ flavor we all love.

1. Combine the shredded chicken, cheddar cheese, cilantro, onion, and BBQ sauce in a medium bowl. Mix to combine.

2. Divide the mixture between 4 tortillas, then tightly roll up the tortillas while folding in the sides like you're creating a burrito.

3. Heat the olive oil in a medium skillet over medium heat. Once the oil is hot, working in batches if necessary, add the wraps to the skillet and brown on each side until golden and crispy, about 5 to 7 minutes.

4. If desired, top with shredded romaine, a dollop of sour cream, and a splash of hot sauce.

Nutrition (per serving):

CALORIES: 308
TOTAL FAT: 17g
TOTAL CARBOHYDRATE: 10g
PROTEIN: 29g

HOWDY-DOING SWEET POTATO SKILLET

PREP TIME: 12 minutes

COOK TIME: 30 minutes

MAKES: 4 servings

SERVING SIZE: ¼ of potatoes

½ tbsp olive oil

1 lb (454g) 95%-lean ground beef

1 large red bell pepper, diced

1 medium red onion, diced

1 tbsp minced garlic (about 4 cloves)

1 (1oz/28g) packet low-sodium taco seasoning

20oz (567g) medium sweet potatoes, peeled and diced

1 (14.5oz/411g) can diced tomatoes

1 cup low-sodium beef broth

½ cup shredded reduced-fat cheddar cheese, for topping

¼ cup chopped fresh cilantro, for topping (optional)

I'm a huge opponent of toxic diet culture and its demonization of carbs. Our bodies need carbs for energy and most importantly cognitive function. Sweet potatoes are a great source of carbs, not only because they are delicious but also because they are packed with nutrients. This delicious Tex-Mex–inspired dish is one that I've made many times on my weight-loss journey.

1. Heat the olive oil in a large skillet over medium heat. Add the ground beef and cook for 5 minutes or until the beef is almost cooked through.

2. Add the bell pepper, onion, and garlic to the skillet. Cook for 3 to 4 minutes or until the vegetables soften. Add 2 tablespoons of water and the taco seasoning to the skillet. Mix well.

3. Transfer the ground beef and vegetable mixture to a bowl and then return the skillet to the heat.

4. Add the sweet potatoes, tomatoes, and beef broth to the skillet. Mix well, cover, and bring to a boil. Once boiling, reduce the heat to low, remove the lid, and simmer for 10 minutes or until the sweet potatoes are cooked through.

5. Add the ground beef and vegetable mixture back to the skillet. Mix well and then remove from the heat. Top with the cheddar cheese and garnish with the cilantro (if using).

Nutrition (per serving):

CALORIES: 332

TOTAL FAT: 7g

TOTAL CARBOHYDRATE: 29g

PROTEIN: 38g

SHRIMP CALIFORNIA ROLL BOWLS

PREP TIME: 15 minutes

COOK TIME: 20 minutes

MAKES: 2 bowls

SERVING SIZE: 1 bowl

This bowl is a deconstructed version of the classic California sushi roll. It's a simple yet light and refreshing meal that offers a mild sweetness and succulence from the shrimp, crunchy freshness from the veggies, and the comforting warmth of a bed of rice to absorb all the flavors.

- 1 cup uncooked sushi rice (short-grain rice)
- 1 tbsp olive oil
- 1 lb (454g) uncooked large shrimp, peeled, deveined, tails removed, and chopped into small pieces
- 1 tbsp garlic powder
- ½ tsp salt
- 1 tsp black pepper
- ¼ cup nonfat plain Greek yogurt
- 2 tbsp sriracha
- 1 tbsp low-sodium soy sauce
- ½ cup diced cucumber
- 1 medium carrot, julienned
- 1 large nori sheet, shredded
- ½ large avocado, diced
- 2 tbsp sesame seeds

1. Place the rice in a mesh strainer. Rinse under cold water until the water runs clear.

2. Add 2 cups of water to a large pot. Bring to a boil over high heat, then add the rice, stir, and reduce heat to low. Cover with a lid and simmer for 15 to 20 minutes or until the water has been absorbed and the rice is tender. Remove from the heat, cover, and set aside to allow the rice to continue to steam for 5 to 10 minutes.

3. Add the olive oil to a medium skillet over medium heat. When the oil is hot, add the shrimp. Sprinkle the garlic powder, salt, and pepper over the shrimp, toss to coat, then cook for 5 to 10 minutes. Remove the shrimp from the skillet and set aside.

4. To a small bowl, add the Greek yogurt, sriracha, and soy sauce. Mix until well combined.

5. Add equal amounts of the rice, cucumber, carrots, nori, avocado, and shrimp to each of two bowls. Top with the sesame seeds and then drizzle the Greek yogurt-sriracha sauce over the top. Enjoy!

Nutrition (per serving):

CALORIES: 475

TOTAL FAT: 18g

TOTAL CARBOHYDRATE: 39g

PROTEIN: 39g

NOTE: I like to add extra nori and soy sauce, but you can adjust the ingredients to suit your tastes.

BEEF CHILI

PREP TIME: 15 minutes

COOK TIME:
50 minutes

MAKES: 4 servings

SERVING SIZE:
¼ of chili

1 tsp olive oil

1 lb (454g) 95%-lean ground beef

1 medium white onion, diced

4 garlic cloves, minced

1 (15.5oz/439g) can kidney beans, drained

1 (14.5oz/411g) can diced tomatoes

2 cups (475ml) beef bone broth

2 tbsp chili powder

2 tsp paprika

1 tsp cumin

1 tsp dried oregano

1 tsp salt

1 tsp black pepper

Nutrition (per serving):

CALORIES: 435

TOTAL FAT: 10g

TOTAL CARBOHYDRATE: 34g

PROTEIN: 53g

NOTES: If desired, add toppings like low-fat sour cream, reduced-fat cheddar cheese, sliced jalapeños, or green onions. I opted to use bone broth for this recipe because it's much higher in protein than regular broth, which in turn helps keep you satiated for longer.

This chili is hearty, easy to make, filling, and great for those busy nights when you don't want to fuss much in the kitchen. You can store leftovers in the fridge to have on hand for a quick grab-and-go lunch or dinner.

1. Heat the olive oil in a deep skillet over medium-high heat. Add the ground beef and brown for 4 minutes, breaking it up as it cooks.

2. To the ground beef, add the onion and garlic. Cook for 3 to 4 minutes or until the onion has softened. Add in the chili, paprika, cumin, oregano, salt, and pepper, and cook for 1 minute until fragrant.

3. Add the kidney beans, diced tomatoes, and bone broth. Stir well and allow to come to a boil.

4. Once the chili is boiling, reduce the heat to low and cover the pot with a lid. Simmer for 30 minutes, then uncover the pot and simmer for 10 minutes more, stirring occasionally, until the chili has thickened.

5. Garnish with your favorite toppings and serve hot.

FIERY CHICKEN BURGER

PREP TIME: 15 minutes

COOK TIME: 20 minutes

MAKES: 1 serving

SERVING SIZE: 1 burger

1 tsp paprika

3 garlic cloves, minced

½ tsp salt

1 tsp black pepper

1 chipotle pepper in adobo sauce, finely chopped

1 tbsp adobo sauce

Juice of ½ lemon

Olive oil cooking spray

1 (8oz/227g) boneless skinless chicken breast, sliced in half horizontally to create two thin slices

1 lower-calorie burger bun (I like Old Tyme 647 burger buns)

2 beefsteak tomato slices

1 iceberg lettuce leaf

1 thin slice Colby Jack cheese

For the avocado spread:

¼ large Hass avocado

½ tsp paprika

½ tsp salt

½ tsp garlic powder

½ tsp black pepper

1 tbsp lemon juice

You can never go wrong with a chicken burger! This burger is made with lean chicken breast and marinated with a chipotle pepper for a bold and fiery flavor. Lower-calorie buns help keep the calories down, and healthy fats help keep you satiated.

1. Make the avocado spread by combining the avocado, paprika, salt, garlic powder, pepper, and lemon juice in a small bowl. Use a fork to mash the ingredients until smooth and well combined. Set aside.

2. Combine the paprika, garlic, salt, pepper, chipotle pepper, adobo sauce, and lemon juice in a medium bowl. Stir to combine, then add the chicken and toss to coat. Set aside to marinate for 10 minutes.

3. Lightly coat a large skillet with the cooking spray and place over medium heat. When the skillet is hot, add the chicken breast slices and cook until golden brown, about 10 to 15 minutes, flipping them every 5 minutes. Set aside.

4. Wipe the skillet clean and place it back over medium heat. Lightly spray burger buns with cooking spray and place them cut sides down in the skillet. Toast until golden brown, about 3 minutes.

5. Assemble the burger by spreading a tablespoon of the avocado spread on the bottom bun. Top with the tomato slices, lettuce leaf, chicken slices, and cheese. Spread 1 tablespoon of the avocado spread on the top bun, then place the top bun on the burger.

Nutrition (per serving):

CALORIES: 510

TOTAL FAT: 18g

TOTAL CARBOHYDRATE: 36g

PROTEIN: 61g

CHAPTER 4

ADS

CHOPPED CHICKPEA SALAD

PREP TIME: 15 minutes

COOK TIME: none

MAKES: 3 servings

SERVING SIZE: ⅓ of salad

1 cup shredded carrots

5 cups chopped red cabbage

1 (15oz/439g) can chickpeas (garbanzo beans), rinsed and drained

½ cup finely chopped fresh cilantro

¼ cup finely chopped green onion

1 medium red bell pepper, diced

¾ cup **Curry Peanut Dressing** (p. 93)

This is the ultimate meal prep salad because it won't get soggy. Salads can be one of the trickier things to meal prep because they often will get soggy as they sit in the fridge, but this colorful salad will hold up beautifully and will only taste better as it marinates in the dressing.

1. Combine all the ingredients in a large bowl. Drizzle the dressing over the top, then toss to combine.

2. Store any leftovers in an airtight container in the fridge for up to 4 days.

Nutrition (per serving):

CALORIES: 369

TOTAL FAT: 3g

TOTAL CARBOHYDRATE: 70g

PROTEIN: 14g

NOTE: This is a vegan salad, but you can add any desired protein to help keep you full for longer.

THE APPLEBOTTOM SALAD

PREP TIME: 10 minutes

COOK TIME:
20 minutes

MAKES: 4 servings

SERVING SIZE:
¼ of salad and 1 fillet

Olive oil cooking spray

4 (5oz/142g) skinless salmon fillets

1 tbsp garlic powder

1 tbsp black pepper

1 tbsp paprika

1 tsp salt

2 medium lemons, sliced

⅓ cup uncooked quinoa

4 cups packed, roughly chopped kale

4 servings **Lemon-Dijon Dressing** (p. 91)

1 large Gala apple, diced

¼ cup pomegranate arils

4 tbsp crumbled fat-free feta cheese

If you know me, you know big salads are my thing. If you're looking for a satisfying, big ol' salad, look no further. This hearty salad gets its impactful flavor from the combination of sweet and acidic ingredients: the apple, pomegranate arils, and citrusy flavor of the dressing all play off one another, resulting in a one-of-a-kind salad. The richness, slight sweetness, and ocean brininess of the salmon really takes this salad over the top.

1. Preheat the oven to 400°F (205°C). Spray a baking pan with olive oil cooking spray.

2. Place the salmon fillets in the prepared baking pan. Season the fillets with the garlic powder, pepper, paprika, and salt. Place 2 to 3 lemon slices on top of the fillets. Bake for 12 to 15 minutes or until the salmon is firm and flakes easily with a fork.

3. While the salmon is baking, rinse the quinoa until the water runs clear, then drain well. Add the quinoa to the saucepan and then add ⅔ cup water. Bring to a boil over medium-high heat, cover with a lid, and reduce the heat to low to bring to a simmer. Cook for 15 minutes or until tender. Rinse and set aside to cool.

4. Add the kale to a large bowl and then drizzle the Lemon-Dijon Dressing over the kale. Massage the kale and dressing together for about 1 to 2 minutes. (Massaging the kale softens it and makes it easier to digest.)

5. Add the apple, pomegranate arils, cooked quinoa, and feta to the kale. Mix well to combine. Divide the salad into 4 separate bowls and then top each bowl with a salmon fillet.

Nutrition (per serving):

CALORIES: 514

TOTAL FAT: 21g

TOTAL CARBOHYDRATE: 25g

PROTEIN: 56g

NOTE: Be sure to rinse the quinoa thoroughly, otherwise it can have a bitter taste due to compounds called *saponins.*

THE BADDIE CAESAR SALAD

PREP TIME: 15 minutes

COOK TIME: 30 minutes

MAKES: 2 servings

SERVING SIZE: ½ of salad

1 tbsp chicken bouillon granules

1 tbsp garlic powder, plus more to season

1 tbsp paprika

1 tbsp prepared mustard

1 tsp salt, plus more to season

1 tsp black pepper, plus more to season

1 tbsp olive oil

2 (8oz/226g) boneless, skinless chicken breasts

2 slices sourdough bread, cut into cubes for croutons (or your croutons of choice)

6 cups roughly chopped romaine lettuce

4 servings **Caesar's Light Delight Dressing** (p. 90)

¼ cup shredded Parmesan cheese

3oz (85g) store-bought fries (I like Alexia House Cut Fries)

Nutrition (per serving):

CALORIES: 426

TOTAL FAT: 16g

TOTAL CARBOHYDRATE: 40g

PROTEIN: 32g

NOTES: If you want to cut down on the cooking time, you can use a rotisserie chicken. (I tend to only use the breast with the skin on for extra flavor.)

I am a Caesar salad addict! You would be surprised at how many different meals you can make with a Caesar salad. What sets this simple salad apart is the fact that it contains healthier alternatives like homemade sourdough croutons and a homemade Caesar dressing.

1. Preheat the oven to 425°F (220°C).

2. Combine the chicken bouillon, garlic powder, paprika, mustard, salt, and pepper in a small bowl. Brush the mixture onto the chicken breasts.

3. Heat the olive oil in a small pan over medium heat. Add the chicken breasts and cook for about 20 minutes or until golden brown and completely cooked through, flipping the chicken halfway through the cooking process.

4. While the chicken is cooking, place the sourdough cubes on a baking tray and lightly season with salt, pepper, and garlic powder. Bake for 10 minutes or until golden brown and crispy. (To make the croutons in the air fryer, air-fry at 400°F [205°C] for 6 minutes.)

5. Once the croutons are baked, transfer them to a plate to cool. Add the fries to the baking sheet and bake according to package instructions, about 20 minutes. (If you wish to use the air fryer to make the fries, air-fry them at 400°F [205°C] for 12 minutes.)

6. When the chicken is done cooking, transfer to a cutting board to cool slightly. Once cooled, slice the chicken into strips.

7. In a large bowl, combine the romaine lettuce, croutons, Caesar's Light Delight Dressing, Parmesan, and fries. Toss to combine and then divide the salad into 2 separate bowls. Top each salad with a sliced chicken breast.

8. Store any leftover salad in an airtight container in the fridge for up to 4 days.

SPRING ROLL SALAD

PREP TIME: 15 minutes

COOK TIME: 10 minutes

MAKES: 4 servings

SERVING SIZE: ¼ of salad

- 1 tbsp olive oil
- 1 lb (454g) large raw shrimp, thawed, peeled, and deveined
- 1 cup vermicelli noodles
- 1 cup shredded carrots
- ½ small head red cabbage, shredded
- 1 medium English cucumber, thinly sliced
- ½ cup finely chopped fresh mint
- ½ cup finely chopped fresh cilantro
- 1–2 fresh jalapeños, seeded and minced
- 6 tbsp **Skinny Peanut Dressing** (p. 101)
- Chili oil (optional)

This is probably one the easiest salads to meal prep in advance. You can prep all the ingredients in advance and then just throw the salad together when you're ready to eat. It's a lifesaver! And we all know that the best part of a spring roll is the peanut dressing, so the accompanying Skinny Peanut Dressing really takes this salad to the next level.

---

1. Add the olive oil to a large skillet over medium heat. Once the oil is hot, add the shrimp to the skillet. Cook on each side for 2 to 3 minutes or until the shrimp are opaque and cooked through.

2. Fill a large pot with water and then bring to a boil over high heat. Once boiling, add the noodles and cook for 3 to 6 minutes or until al dente. Drain and rinse in cold water. Set aside to drain.

3. To a large bowl, add the carrots, cabbage, cucumber, mint, cilantro, jalapeños (more or less, depending on your preferences), shrimp, and cooked rice noodles. Drizzle the dressing over the top and then mix well. Top with a drizzle of chili oil (if using).

4. Store in an airtight container in the fridge for up to 4 days.

Nutrition (per serving):

CALORIES: 181

TOTAL FAT: 2g

TOTAL CARBOHYDRATE: 17g

PROTEIN: 17g

WARM BROCCOLI CRUNCH SALAD

PREP TIME: 10 minutes

COOK TIME: 20 minutes

MAKES: 3 servings

SERVING SIZE: ⅓ of salad

2 cups chopped fresh broccoli florets
1 cup chopped carrots
½ cup chopped white onion
½ tsp salt
½ tsp black pepper
1 tbsp olive oil
1 (15.5oz/439g) can chickpeas, drained and rinsed
¼ cup sunflower kernels
2 cups spring lettuce mix
6 tbsp **Hummus Dressing** (p. 97)

When I began my weight-loss journey, I discovered warm salads and my life was forever changed. I was mind-blown. Serving salad warm is a simple and delicious concept that really elevates the flavor. And when it comes to warm salads, I love using baked broccoli as a base because it's filling and is one of those vegetables that really absorbs flavors well.

1. Preheat the oven at 400°F (205°C). Line a rimmed baking sheet with parchment paper.

2. Place the broccoli, carrots, and onion in an even layer on the prepared baking sheet. Season with salt and pepper, and then lightly drizzle olive oil over the veggies. Bake for 15 to 20 minutes or until tender.

3. In a large salad bowl, combine the cooked veggies, chickpeas, sunflower kernels, and spring lettuce mix. Drizzle the hummus dressing over the top. Toss to coat and enjoy.

4. Store any leftovers in an airtight container in the fridge for up to 4 days.

Nutrition (per serving):

CALORIES: 265
TOTAL FAT: 13g
TOTAL CARBOHYDRATE: 30g
PROTEIN: 12g

NOTE: To make this delicious salad a full meal, I recommend serving it with a grilled chicken breast. (I like to dice the chicken breast and add it to the salad.)

SALMON SUSHI SALAD

PREP TIME: 10 minutes

COOK TIME:
10 minutes

MAKES: 1 serving

SERVING SIZE: 1 salad

1 (6oz/227g) skin-on salmon fillet

½ tsp salt

1 tsp garlic powder

1 tsp onion powder

1 tsp paprika

1 tsp black pepper

Olive oil

1 cup cooked jasmine rice, warm

½ medium avocado, diced

½ large cucumber, sliced

2 green onions, sliced

2 small nori sheets, shredded

3 tbsp **Tahini-Soy Dressing** (p. 100)

Sesame seeds, for topping (optional)

Pickled ginger, for serving (optional)

Sriracha, for topping (optional)

You might want to fight me because I'm calling this a "salad" even though there are no leafy greens in the recipe, but who says I can't call it a salad? I took everything I love about sushi and combined it all, resulting in one of the most delicious and satisfying salads you'll ever taste.

1. Season the salmon fillet with salt, garlic powder, onion powder, paprika, and pepper.

2. Add a drizzle of olive oil to a skillet placed over medium heat. Once the oil is hot, add the salmon fillet and cook for 7 to 10 minutes on each side (depending on the thickness of the fish) or until the fish is cooked through. Set aside.

3. Remove the skin from the salmon fillet and then use a fork to shred. Add the warm cooked rice and salmon to a serving bowl and then mix well to combine. Add the avocado, cucumber, spring onions, and nori. Toss gently to combine.

4. Drizzle the dressing over the salad, sprinkle the sesame seeds (if using) over the top, and add the pickled ginger (if using) on the side. Top with a drizzle of sriracha (if using).

5. Store any leftovers in an airtight container in the fridge for up to 4 days.

Nutrition (per serving):

CALORIES: 717

TOTAL FAT: 29g

TOTAL CARBOHYDRATE: 57g

PROTEIN: 55g

BURRITO SALAD

PREP TIME: 10 minutes

COOK TIME:
10 minutes

MAKES: 2 servings

SERVING SIZE:
½ of salad

1 tbsp olive oil

8oz (227g) 95%-lean
ground beef

1 (1oz/28g) package taco
seasoning

1 cup microwavable
Spanish-style rice (I like
Ben's Original Ready Rice)

4 cups chopped romaine
lettuce

1 medium avocado, diced

1 cup chopped fresh cilantro

2 large Roma tomatoes,
chopped

½ small red onion, minced

1 cup black beans, rinsed and
drained

4 tbsp **Fiesta Dressing** (p. 98)

If turning anything to a salad was a sport, I'd be a gold medal
Olympian. This burrito salad has everything you love about a
burrito, but without the tortilla and extra-fat ingredients. I make
this with leaner ground beef, which cuts out a substantial amount
of the fat. You already know I am not against carbs, so I added a
little bit of rice into the recipe to complete it.

1. Add the olive oil to a large skillet over medium heat. When the oil is hot, add
the ground beef and taco seasoning. Use a wooden spoon to break up the
meat and mix the ingredients together. Cook until the ground beef is
cooked through. Set aside.

2. Microwave the rice as instructed on the package. Set aside.

3. To a large salad bowl, add the romaine lettuce, rice, ground beef, avocado,
cilantro, tomatoes, onion, and black beans. Drizzle the dressing over the
top and toss to combine.

Nutrition (per serving):

CALORIES: 529

TOTAL FAT: 17g

TOTAL CARBOHYDRATE: 47g

PROTEIN: 36g

BUFFALO CHICKEN SALAD

COOK TIME:
30 minutes

PREP TIME: 10 minutes

MAKES: 4 servings

SERVING SIZE:
¼ of salad

1 lb (454g) boneless, skinless chicken breasts

¼ cup Frank's RedHot sauce

½ tsp ground cumin

½ tsp paprika

½ tsp garlic powder

½ tsp onion powder

Salt, to taste

Black pepper, to taste

3 tbsp olive oil, divided

½ medium red onion, sliced

4 cups chopped romaine lettuce

2 medium carrots, shredded

½ medium cucumber, peeled and diced

½ cup halved cherry tomatoes

¼ cup canned corn, drained

¼ cup crumbled reduced-fat blue cheese

6 tbsp **Jalapeño-Lime Ranch Dressing** (p. 92)

I'm a sucker for anything buffalo flavored, so I knew I just had to come up with a salad that incorporated buffalo chicken. This salad offers a delicious combination of spicy, tangy, and refreshing flavors; it's so delicious that it's remained a favorite go-to for me for quite a while now.

1. Place the chicken breasts in a medium bowl.

2. In a small bowl, combine the Frank's RedHot sauce, cumin, paprika, garlic powder, and onion powder. Stir to combine and then season to taste with salt and black pepper. Pour the sauce over the chicken breasts.

3. Heat 2 tablespoons of the olive oil in a large skillet over medium-low heat. Once the oil is hot, add the chicken breasts and cook for about 20 minutes or until golden brown and completely cooked through, flipping the breasts halfway through the cooking process. Remove the chicken breasts from the skillet and set aside to cool slightly before slicing into strips.

4. Add the remaining 1 tablespoon of olive oil to the hot skillet. Add the onion and sauté until tender and golden brown.

5. To a large bowl, add the romaine lettuce, carrots, cucumber, tomatoes, corn, sliced chicken breast, sautéed onion, and blue cheese. Drizzle the dressing over the top and then toss well.

6. Store any leftover salad in an airtight container in the fridge for up to 2 days.

Nutrition (per serving):

CALORIES: 349

TOTAL FAT: 18g

TOTAL CARBOHYDRATE: 9g

PROTEIN: 36g

DRES

CAESAR'S LIGHT DELIGHT DRESSING

PREP TIME: 5 minutes

COOK TIME: none

MAKES: 1 cup

SERVING SIZE: ¼ cup

2 garlic cloves
2 tbsp lemon juice
2 anchovy fillets
2 tsp Worcestershire sauce
½ cup nonfat Greek yogurt
1 tsp Dijon mustard
¼ cup grated Parmesan
   cheese
Salt, to taste
Black pepper, to taste

Traditional dressings use a base of olive oil which can really skyrocket the calories and easily put you out of your deficit. This dressing still has all the tasty ingredients of a traditional Caesar dressing, but the Greek yogurt makes it higher in protein and creamier.

1. Combine all the ingredients in a blender. Blend until completely smooth.

2. Store in an airtight container in the refrigerator for up to 5 days.

Nutrition (per serving):

CALORIES: 47

TOTAL FAT: 2g

TOTAL CARBOHYDRATE: 2g

PROTEIN: 5g

LEMON-DIJON DRESSING

PREP TIME: 2 minutes

COOK TIME: none

MAKES: ⅓ cup

SERVING SIZE: 2 tablespoons

3 tbsp lemon juice
1 tsp honey
1 tsp Dijon mustard
2 tbsp nonfat Greek yogurt
1 tsp olive oil
Salt, to taste
¼ tsp salt
¼ tsp black pepper
¼ tsp garlic powder

This traditional homemade dressing is made with my favorite hack for not only making dressings healthier but lower calorie—Greek yogurt! This dressing is undoubtedly one of my favorites. I find it works well with many different types of salads; it's sweet, yet it has a bright and citrusy undertone from the lemon juice that really compliments the rest of the salad ingredients.

1. Combine the ingredients in a jar. Cover the jar tightly and shake until combined.
2. Store in the refrigerator for up to 5 days.

Nutrition (per serving):

CALORIES: 156
TOTAL FAT: 8g
TOTAL CARBOHYDRATE: 14g
PROTEIN: 8g

JALAPEÑO-LIME RANCH DRESSING

PREP TIME: 5 minutes

COOK TIME: none

MAKES: 1 cup

SERVING SIZE: 2 tablespoons

¾ cup chopped fresh cilantro leaves

½ cup pickled jalapeños

¾ cup of nonfat Greek yogurt

¼ cup low-calorie milk of your choice (I use unsweetened almond milk)

1 tbsp dry ranch seasoning

1 tsp garlic powder

½ tsp salt

2 tbsp pickled jalapeño juice

1 tbsp lime juice

This dressing is a creamy fusion of ranch and spicy jalapeños, with a refreshing burst of lime. It has a classic ranch base made from ranch seasoning and nonfat Greek yogurt to help keep you in a deficit. The pickled jalapeños give this dressing a subtle yet exciting kick of heat. The lime juice really brings it all together by balancing the creamy and spicy elements.

1. In a food processor or blender, blend the cilantro leaves and pickled jalapeños.

2. In a medium mixing bowl, mix the Greek yogurt, milk, ranch seasoning, garlic powder, salt, jalapeño juice, and lime juice.

3. Add the cilantro and jalapeño mixture to the bowl along with the other ingredients. Mix well.

4. Store in an airtight container in the refrigerator for up to 5 days.

Nutrition (per serving):

CALORIES: 38

TOTAL FAT: 3g

TOTAL CARBOHYDRATE: 0g

PROTEIN: 4g

NOTES: Pickled jalapeños have a tangy flavor with a moderate level of heat. I think they add just the right amount of heat to this dressing, but feel free to adjust to suit your tastes. This dressing is incredibly diverse, as it pairs well with many dishes like salads, tacos, burritos, grilled meats, and vegetable platters for dipping.

CURRY PEANUT DRESSING

PREP TIME: 5 minutes

COOK TIME: none

MAKES: ¾ cup

SERVING SIZE: 2 tablespoons

¼ cup creamy peanut butter
1 tbsp grated fresh ginger
1 garlic clove, minced
1 tbsp lemon juice
2 tbsp low-sodium soy sauce
1 tsp yellow curry powder
1 tsp onion powder
Salt, to taste
Black pepper, to taste

This is a flavor bomb of a dressing. Peanut butter has the potential to make delicious dressings when paired with the right ingredients. This dressing is creamy and has a full-bodied flavor that will complement the Chopped Chickpea Salad (p. 74). This dressing will also pair well with other Asian-inspired salads, and you can even use it as a dip for spring rolls.

1. In a medium bowl, combine the peanut butter, ginger, garlic, lemon juice, soy sauce, curry powder, onion powder. Whisk until smooth.

2. Add 3 to 4 tablespoons of warm water to thin the dressing into a pourable consistency. Season to taste with salt and pepper.

3. Store any leftover dressing in an airtight container in the fridge for up to 4 days.

Nutrition (per serving):

CALORIES: 132
TOTAL FAT: 11g
TOTAL CARBOHYDRATE: 6g
PROTEIN: 5g

PESTO DRESSING

PREP TIME: 5 minutes

COOK TIME: none

MAKES: ¼ cup

SERVING SIZE:
2 tablespoons

3 tbsp plain nonfat Greek
   yogurt
2 tbsp store-bought pesto
   sauce
1 tsp honey
¼ tsp garlic powder
Salt, to taste
Black pepper, to taste

This is probably one of the simplest dressings you can make, but it's packed full of flavor thanks to the pesto. I am a pesto lover, but it can be on the higher side of calories, so I knew I needed to come up with a recipe that could stretch out the pesto without compromising flavor. This dressing is perfect for salads or even drizzled over protein pasta.

1. Combine all the dressing ingredients in a resealable container. Shake or stir until well combined.

2. Add a small amount of water and then shake or stir again until combined. (You'll want to add only enough water to make the dressing a pourable consistency.)

3. Store any leftover dressing in the fridge for up to 4 days.

Nutrition (per serving):

CALORIES: 103
TOTAL FAT: 8g
TOTAL CARBOHYDRATE: 4g
PROTEIN: 4g

LEMON VINAIGRETTE

PREP TIME: 5 minutes

COOK TIME: none

MAKES: 1½ cups

SERVING SIZE: 2 tablespoons

¾ cup extra-virgin olive oil
½ cup lemon juice
  (about 4 lemons)
2 garlic cloves, minced
1 tsp Dijon mustard
1 tbsp honey
Salt, to taste
Black pepper, to taste

When I started my weight-loss journey, a simple vinaigrette was the first thing I learned to make. This is an all-time classic salad dressing that you can prep and keep on hand at all times. It is simple to make and such an easy way to add flavor to your salads. With olive oil being the base, it can be calorie dense, but olive oil used in moderation is very good for your health—it can help support heart health and has anti-inflammatory properties.

1. To a 2-cup jar, add the olive oil, lemon juice, garlic, Dijon mustard, and honey. Seal the jar tightly and shake vigorously to combine. Season to taste with salt and pepper.

2. Store in an airtight container in the fridge for up to 5 days.

Nutrition (per serving):

CALORIES: 193
TOTAL FAT: 21g
TOTAL CARBOHYDRATE: 4g
PROTEIN: 0g

TAHINI-SRIRACHA DRESSING

PREP TIME: 5 minutes

COOK TIME: none

MAKES: ½ cup

SERVING SIZE:
2 tablespoons

3 tbsp low-sodium soy sauce
2 tbsp sriracha
2 tbsp tahini paste
½ tsp sesame oil

This dressing is tangy and slightly spicy, making it the perfect companion to the Salmon Sushi Salad or any other salad that calls for a dressing with a kick. Sriracha contains antioxidants which can help reduce inflammation and boost your metabolism.

1. Combine the ingredients in a small bowl. Whisk until smooth.

2. Store any leftover dressing in an airtight container for up to 4 days.

Nutrition (per serving):

CALORIES: 154
TOTAL FAT: 10g
TOTAL CARBOHYDRATE: 12g
PROTEIN: 7g

HUMMUS DRESSING

PREP TIME: 5 minutes

COOK TIME: none

MAKES: ¾ cup

SERVING SIZE:
2 tablespoons

½ cup roasted garlic hummus
   (I like Sabra brand)
1 tsp white wine vinegar
1 tbsp extra-virgin olive oil
2 tbsp lemon juice
2 tbsp water
1 tbsp honey
Salt, to taste
Black pepper, to taste

This dressing is so good you'll want to drink it! Using hummus as the base makes for such a flavorful and impactful dressing. Roasted garlic hummus is hands down one of my favorite dips, and transforming it into a dressing has made eating healthy so much easier.

1. To a medium bowl, add all the dressing ingredients. Whisk until a smooth and pourable consistency is achieved.

2. Store any leftover dressing in an airtight container in the fridge for up to 4 days.

Nutrition (per serving):

CALORIES: 40
TOTAL FAT: 3g
TOTAL CARBOHYDRATE: 3g
PROTEIN: 0g

FIESTA DRESSING

PREP TIME: 5 minutes
COOK TIME: none
MAKES: 4 servings
SERVING SIZE: ¼ cup

1 cup plain nonfat Greek yogurt
¾ tsp paprika
¾ tsp chili powder
1 tsp onion powder
1 tsp garlic powder
1 tsp ground cumin
1 tsp apple cider vinegar

I love using Greek yogurt as a base for my dressings—it makes the dressings creamy and much healthier. Greek yogurt has probiotics to support gut health and cuts down on the fat and calories that most dressings have. This dressing pairs well with many different types of salads but I love adding it to any Southwestern-inspired recipes.

1. Combine all the ingredients in a resealable container or jar. Mix until all the ingredients are well combined and completely smooth.
2. Cover tightly and store in the fridge for up to 4 days.

Nutrition (per serving):

CALORIES: 39
TOTAL FAT: 74g
TOTAL CARBOHYDRATE: 0g
PROTEIN: 6g

SPICY RANCH DRESSING

PREP TIME: 5 minutes

COOK TIME: none

MAKES: ½ cup

SERVING SIZE: 2 tablespoons

½ cup nonfat plain Greek yogurt

1 tbsp hot sauce (I use Frank's RedHot sauce)

1 tbsp lemon juice

¼ tsp garlic powder

¼ tsp onion powder

1 tsp honey

¼ tsp dried dill

Salt, to taste

Ranch dressing is universal: It's used as a dressing for salads, a dip for veggies, and as a condiment for dishes like chicken wings, sandwiches, and wraps. I've put a spicy spin on this American staple to really elevate my salads, while still keeping the dressing low calorie and healthy.

1. In a small bowl, combine the Greek yogurt, hot sauce, lemon juice, garlic powder, onion powder, honey, and dried dill. Whisk until smooth, then season to taste with salt.

2. Add water in small amounts until a pourable consistency is achieved.

3. Store any leftover dressing in an airtight container in the fridge for up to 4 days

Nutrition (per serving):

CALORIES: 28

TOTAL FAT: 0g

TOTAL CARBOHYDRATE: 4g

PROTEIN: 3g

NOTE: If you aren't a fan of spicy dressings, you can omit the hot sauce.

TAHINI-SOY DRESSING

PREP TIME: 5 minutes

COOK TIME: none

MAKES: ½ cup

SERVING SIZE: 2 tablespoons

3 tbsp low-sodium soy sauce
2 tbsp tahini paste
1 tsp sesame oil
1 tbsp honey
¼ tsp garlic powder

This Asian-inspired dressing is creamy and sweet and has been one of my hyperfixation dressings for a while. Tahini, a paste made from ground sesame seeds, is what makes this dressing so creamy and gives it a distinct deep, earthy, nutty flavor. The nuttiness is similar to that of other seed butters, like peanut butter or almond butter.

1. Combine all the ingredients in a medium bowl. Whisk until smooth.
2. Store any leftovers in an airtight container in the fridge for up to 4 days.

Nutrition (per serving):

CALORIES: 168
TOTAL FAT: 10g
TOTAL CARBOHYDRATE: 15g
PROTEIN: 7g

SKINNY PEANUT DRESSING

PREP TIME: 5 minutes

COOK TIME: none

MAKES: ⅓ cup

SERVING SIZE:
2 tablespoons

⅓ cup low-calorie powdered peanut butter (I like PBfit brand)
1 tbsp extra-virgin olive oil
1 tbsp low-sodium soy sauce
1 tbsp honey
1 tsp rice vinegar
1 garlic clove, minced
1 tsp grated fresh ginger
Juice of ½ a lime

The peanut butter in this recipe makes the creamiest dressing, without the need to add any dairy. Similar dressings are used in Asian cuisine, and what I love about this dressing is that it can be used to dress salads, noodles, or as a dipping sauce for various dishes.

1. In a medium bowl, combine the peanut butter powder with 2 to 3 tablespoons of water until a creamy consistency is achieved.

2. To the same bowl, add the olive oil, soy sauce, honey, rice vinegar, garlic, ginger, and lime juice. Whisk until all the ingredients are combined.

3. Store any leftovers in an airtight container in the fridge for up to 4 days.

Nutrition (per serving):

CALORIES: 125
TOTAL FAT: 6g
TOTAL CARBOHYDRATE: 10g
PROTEIN: 7g

CHAPTER 6

BROCCOLI CHEDDAR SOUP

PREP TIME: 15 minutes

COOK TIME: 25 minutes

MAKES: 4 servings

SERVING SIZE: 2 cups

1 cup low-fat cottage cheese
2 tsp olive oil
1½ cups chopped yellow onion
2 tsp minced fresh garlic
⅓ cup all-purpose flour
2½ cups 1% milk
3 cups low-sodium chicken broth
6 cups broccoli florets
1 cup peeled and shredded carrots
1 tsp salt
1 tsp black pepper
¼ tsp nutmeg
1 bay leaf
8oz (227g) shredded reduced-fat sharp cheddar cheese, divided

This hearty soup is one you'll be able to enjoy without guilt! Traditionally, broccoli cheddar soup is loaded in calories from all the butter, cheese, and cream it includes. This recipe, however, is higher in protein because of the cottage cheese and lower in calories and fat because I've swapped in reduced-fat ingredients.

1. Add the cottage cheese to a food processor or blender. Process until smooth. Set aside.

2. Add the olive oil to a large pot over medium heat. When the oil is hot, add the onion. Cook until softened, then add the garlic and cook until fragrant, about 1 minute more. Slowly add the flour to the pot while stirring continuously until a paste is formed. Remove the pot from the heat and allow the paste to cool for 1 minute.

3. Place the pot back over the heat and slowly pour in the milk while stirring continuously. Whisk to smooth out any lumps, then pour in the chicken broth and add the broccoli, carrots, salt, pepper, nutmeg, and bay leaf. Cover and simmer until the carrots and broccoli are tender, about 8 minutes.

4. Uncover the pot and reduce the heat to low. Remove the bay leaf and add the blended cottage cheese and ¾ cup of the cheddar cheese. Stir until the cheese is melted, then transfer half the mixture to a blender.

5. Working in 2 batches, blend the soup until smooth and then add it back to the pot. (Note: tilt the lid on the blender slightly open to ensure the hot soup does not splatter after blending.)

6. Heat the soup for 3 minutes or until hot. Remove the soup from the heat and sprinkle the remaining ¼ cup of cheddar cheese over the top. Serve hot.

7. Store any leftovers in an airtight container in the fridge for up to 4 days.

Nutrition (per serving):

CALORIES: 417
TOTAL FAT: 15g
TOTAL CARBOHYDRATE: 37g
PROTEIN: 20g

CHICKEN ENCHILADA SOUP

PREP TIME: 10 minutes

COOK TIME: 25 minutes

MAKES: 8 servings

SERVING SIZE: 2 cups

1 tbsp olive oil

1 tsp ground cumin

1 tbsp chili powder

3 garlic cloves, minced

¼ cup tomato paste

1 medium white onion, diced

1 large red bell pepper, diced

2 celery stalks, diced

4 cups low-sodium chicken broth

1 (14.5oz/411g) can diced tomatoes

1 tbsp salt

1 tsp dried oregano

Black pepper, to taste

3 (each about 6oz/170g) boneless, skinless chicken breasts

1 (15oz/425g) can black beans, rinsed and drained

1 (4oz/113g) can mild chopped green chiles

1 (15.25oz/432g) can whole kernel corn, drained

½ cup low-fat sour cream

1 cup Mexican-blend cheese, for topping, divided

½ medium Hass avocado, diced, for topping, divided

This chicken enchilada soup is so easy to throw together. It's loaded with hearty shredded chicken and beans, making it a crowd-pleaser. This is a comforting and flavorful dish inspired by all the flavors of traditional Mexican enchiladas.

1. Heat the olive oil in a large pot over medium-high heat. Add the cumin, chili powder, and garlic. Cook for 1 minute until fragrant. Add the tomato paste, stir to combine with the spices, and cook for 2 minutes. Add the onion, bell pepper, and celery. Sauté until the vegetables have softened.

2. Add the chicken broth, diced tomatoes, salt, and oregano. Season to taste with pepper. Bring to a boil and then reduce the heat to low. Add the chicken breasts, cover, and simmer for 15 minutes or until the chicken is cooked. Remove the chicken from the pot, shred with forks, then return the shredded chicken to the pot.

3. Add the black beans, green chiles, corn, and sour cream. Stir to combine and then simmer for another 5 to 10 minutes or until hot. Top each serving with cheese and avocado.

4. Store any leftovers in an airtight container in the fridge for up to 4 days.

Nutrition (per serving):

CALORIES: 340

TOTAL FAT: 7g

TOTAL CARBOHYDRATE: 44g

PROTEIN: 26g

HEARTY LENTIL MEDLEY

PREP TIME: 20 minutes

COOK TIME: 40 minutes

MAKES: 6 servings

SERVING SIZE: 2 cups

3 tbsp olive oil

2 celery stalks, diced

1 medium yellow onion, diced

2 medium carrots, peeled and diced

2 tsp salt

4 garlic cloves, minced

1 tsp paprika

1 tsp turmeric powder

½ tsp black pepper

½ tsp cayenne

½ tsp cumin

8 cups low-sodium vegetable broth

3 cups butternut squash, peeled and diced

1¼ cups uncooked brown lentils, rinsed

2 (14.5oz/411g) cans fire-roasted tomatoes

2 bay leaves

2 cups chopped kale, rinsed and dried

¼ cup lemon juice

Lentil soup is a nutritious and hearty dish made primarily of lentils, which are high in protein and fiber. This soup is made with an abundance of good-for-you veggies and a blend of flavorful spices. It is super simple to make and makes a great meal prep.

1. Heat the olive oil in a large pot over medium heat. Once the oil is hot, add the celery, onion, and carrots. Sauté until the vegetables have softened, about 5 minutes.

2. Add the salt, garlic, paprika, turmeric, pepper, cayenne, and cumin. Stir to combine the veggies with the spices. Cook for 1 minute.

3. Add the vegetable broth, butternut squash, lentils, fire-roasted tomatoes, and bay leaves to the pot. Stir and then increase the heat to medium-high. When the mixture reaches a boil, cover and reduce the heat to medium-low. Simmer for 30 minutes or until the lentils are tender.

4. Remove the bay leaves and add the chopped kale and lemon juice. Stir to combine. Serve hot and enjoy.

5. Store any leftovers in an airtight container in the fridge for up to 4 days.

Nutrition (per serving):

CALORIES: 138

TOTAL FAT: 8g

TOTAL CARBOHYDRATE: 16g

PROTEIN: 2g

LASAGNA SOUP

PREP TIME: 10 minutes

COOK TIME: 40 minutes

MAKES: 5 servings

SERVING SIZE: 2 cups

10oz (284g) low-fat cottage cheese

1 tbsp olive oil

1 lb (454g) 95%-lean ground beef

1 tsp salt

1 tbsp black pepper

1 medium yellow onion, diced

5 garlic cloves, minced

2 tbsp tomato paste

1 (24oz/680g) jar low-sugar marinara sauce

1 tsp Italian seasoning

1 tsp onion powder

1 bay leaf

4 cups beef bone broth

3 large lasagna sheets, broken into small pieces

2 large zucchini, halved lengthwise and thinly sliced

¼ cup chopped fresh basil, plus more for serving

½ cup grated Parmesan cheese, plus more for serving

Crusty bread, for serving (optional)

This soup is a delicious and comforting twist on the classic Italian pasta dish and features all the flavors of traditional lasagna. I was able to reduce the calories and fat in this soup by making a few substitutions like using leaner ground beef and low-sugar marinara. With that said, I refused to cut out the pasta because I'm a pasta lover and also a believer that everything in moderation is okay.

1. Blend the cottage cheese in a food processor until smooth. Set aside.

2. Heat the olive oil in a large pot over medium heat. When the oil is hot, add the ground beef and season with the salt and black pepper. Cook for 10 minutes or until browned, using a wooden spoon to break up the meat.

3. Remove the meat from the pot and add the diced onion. Sauté until the onion has softened, then add the garlic, tomato paste, marinara sauce, Italian seasoning, onion powder, bay leaf, bone broth, and blended cottage cheese. Add 1 cup of water to the marinara sauce jar, swirl to incorporate the remaining sauce with the water, then add it to the pot. Stir again, add the meat back to the pot, then stir once more.

4. Bring to a boil, then add the lasagna pieces and reduce the heat to medium-low. Cook until the lasagna pieces are tender, about 10 minutes.

5. Once the pasta is tender, add the zucchini. Stir to combine, cover, and cook for about 1 to 2 minutes or until the zucchini is tender. Remove from the heat and stir in basil and Parmesan. Remove the bay leaf.

6. If desired, serve with extra basil, extra Parmesan, and crusty bread.

7. Store any leftovers in an airtight container in the fridge for up to 4 days.

Nutrition (per serving):

CALORIES: 509

TOTAL FAT: 53g

TOTAL CARBOHYDRATE: 32g

PROTEIN: 53g

NOTES: If you wish to make this dish higher in protein, you can replace the lasagna sheets with protein pasta. If you wish to leave the pasta out entirely, you can double the zucchini.

ZUPPA TOSCANA

PREP TIME: 10 minutes

COOK TIME: 30 minutes

MAKES: 5 servings

SERVING SIZE: 1½ cups

1 tbsp olive oil

1 lb (454g) Italian-style ground turkey sausage

8 slices turkey bacon, diced

1 medium yellow onion, diced

2 garlic cloves, minced

4 medium russet potatoes, peeled and diced

2 tsp Italian seasoning

6 cups low-sodium chicken broth

1 tbsp cornstarch

½ cup low-fat sour cream

½ bunch kale, rinsed, dried, and chopped

Salt, to taste

Black pepper, to taste

2 tsp crushed red pepper flakes, for topping (optional)

Zuppa Toscana, or "Tuscan Soup," is a popular soup inspired by ingredients typically found in the Tuscan countryside. This hearty soup traditionally uses Italian pork sausage, but I've replaced that with Italian turkey sausage to lighten up this delicious soup. I'm a believer that you can make any dish lighter without compromising flavor by making a few substitutions, and that is exactly what I've accomplished with this classic.

1. Add the olive oil to a large pot over medium heat. When the oil is hot, add the sausage and cook until the sausage is fully cooked. Remove the sausage from the pot to a paper towel-lined plate to drain. Add the turkey bacon to the pot. Cook until the bacon is browned and fully cooked, then transfer the bacon to the plate with the turkey. (Reserve some of the bacon for topping.)

2. To the same pot, add the onion and garlic. Cook until softened.

3. Add the potatoes, Italian seasoning, and chicken broth. Boil the potatoes until fork-tender, about 12 minutes.

4. While the potatoes are cooking, combine the cornstarch and 2 tablespoons of cold water in a small bowl. Stir to create a slurry. Add the slurry to the soup while stirring to thicken.

5. Stir in the turkey sausage, turkey bacon (reserving some for topping), sour cream, and kale. Season to taste with salt and pepper. Sprinkle the red pepper flakes (if using) over the soup and enjoy!

6. Store any leftovers in an airtight container in the fridge for up to 4 days.

Nutrition (per serving):

CALORIES: 429

TOTAL FAT: 29g

TOTAL CARBOHYDRATE: 27g

PROTEIN: 21g

VER

SLOW COOKER SHREDDED BEEF

PREP TIME: 20 minutes

COOK TIME: 8 hours

MAKES: 3 servings

SERVING SIZE:
⅓ of chuck roast

2 large Roma tomatoes

½ medium white onion

4 garlic cloves, peeled

2 tbsp chicken bouillon granules

1 tsp black pepper

1 tsp ground cumin

1 tbsp garlic powder

1 tbsp onion powder

1 tbsp paprika

1 tbsp dried oregano

1 tbsp dried thyme

½ tsp salt

1 tbsp apple cider vinegar

1 (32 fl oz/907g) carton low-sodium beef broth

1 lb (454g) chuck roast

2 bay leaves

This is probably one of the most versatile recipes I make because you can make it into so many other dishes. I was inspired to make this by the traditional Mexican recipe of birria, which is a meat stew most famously known for being made into tacos.

1. Add the tomatoes, onion, garlic cloves, and 2 cups of water (or enough to cover the vegetables) to a medium pot over medium-high heat. Bring to a boil, then lower the heat to medium-low. Simmer uncovered for about 6 minutes or until everything has softened. Once cooked, drain the water from the pot.

2. Add the cooked tomatoes, onion, and garlic and the chicken bouillon, pepper, cumin, garlic powder, onion powder, paprika, oregano, thyme, salt, apple cider vinegar, and beef broth to a blender. Blend until smooth.

3. Add the chuck roast to a slow cooker and then strain the blended seasoning mixture over the chuck roast until completely covered. Discard the solids. Top with 2 bay leaves, cover, and cook on low for 7 to 8 hours (or on high for 3 to 4 hours) until tender.

4. Once the meat is cooked, discard the bay leaves and remove the meat from the slow cooker. Shred the meat with forks, then add it back to the cooking liquid. Stir to combine. Enjoy on top of salads, burrito bowls, or tacos.

Nutrition (per serving):

CALORIES: 363

TOTAL FAT: 14g

TOTAL CARBOHYDRATE: 4g

PROTEIN: 50g

NOTE: If you're in a hurry, you can cook the beef on high for 3 to 4 hours, but it won't be as tender as it would be if it was cooked on low.

AIR-FRIED SHREDDED BEEF TAQUITOS

PREP TIME: 10 minutes

COOK TIME: 12 minutes

MAKES: 15 taquitos

SERVING SIZE:
5 taquitos

2 cups **Slow Cooker Shredded Beef** (p. 116), drained

1 cup fat-free shredded cheddar cheese

Salt, to taste

15 medium corn tortillas (I like Mission Yellow Corn Tortillas)

Olive oil cooking spray

½ cup diced white onion, for topping (optional)

4 tbsp low-fat sour cream, for topping (optional)

4 tbsp green salsa, for topping (optional)

⅓ cup guacamole, for topping (optional)

I grew up eating deep-fried taquitos of all kinds, so when I began eating healthier, I knew I had to figure out a way to still eat taquitos without all the oil. Thankfully, my air fryer saved the day!

1. To a large bowl, add the shredded beef and cheddar cheese. Mix well and then season to taste with salt.

2. Wrap the tortillas in a damp paper towel and heat in the microwave for 30 seconds, or heat the tortillas in a skillet over high heat for 1 minute to soften.

3. Add 2 heaping tablespoons of the shredded beef mixture to each tortilla and then tightly roll it up. Repeat with the remaining ingredients. Place the taquitos seam-sides down in the air fryer. Spray with olive oil cooking spray and air-fry at 390°F (200°C) for 8 to 12 minutes or until crispy and golden brown.

4. Add toppings such as low-fat sour cream, green salsa, onion, or guacamole. Enjoy the crunch!

Nutrition (per serving):

CALORIES: 300

TOTAL FAT: 4g

TOTAL CARBOHYDRATE: 45g

PROTEIN: 22g

NOTE: If you don't have an air fryer, you can bake these taquitos in the oven at 400°F (205°C) for 20 minutes.

CHICKEN FAJITA MAC AND CHEESE

PREP TIME: 10 minutes

COOK TIME: 15 minutes

MAKES: 4 servings

SERVING SIZE: ¼ of mac and cheese

20oz (567g) boneless, skinless chicken breast, cut into ½- to ¾-inch cubes

1 (1oz/28g) packet fajita seasoning

8oz (227g) high-protein elbow macaroni (I like Barilla Protein+ Macaroni)

1 tbsp olive oil

1 red bell pepper, diced

½ small white onion, diced

1½ cups low-fat cottage cheese

½ cup reduced-fat cheddar cheese

½ cup 2% milk

1 packet mac and cheese powder (I use Kraft brand)

1 tsp garlic powder

½ tsp black pepper

My weakness has always been mac and cheese, so I knew I had to make a healthier alternative. This recipe is so delicious and tastes like regular mac and cheese. It's also packed full of flavor and protein. The protein pasta, cottage cheese, reduced-fat cheese, and low-fat milk all keep things lighter. (And before you ask, no, you can't taste the cottage cheese!)

1. Add the chicken and fajita seasoning to a medium bowl. Toss the chicken to coat.

2. Cook the protein macaroni until al dente, about 10 minutes. Drain and set aside.

3. Add the olive oil to a large skillet over medium heat. When the oil is hot, add the chicken and cook, stirring occasionally, for 5 minutes, then add the bell pepper and onion. Continue cooking for 5 minutes more or until the chicken and veggies are fully cooked. Set aside.

4. To a blender, add the cottage cheese, cheddar cheese, milk, mac and cheese powder, garlic powder, and pepper. Blend until smooth.

5. Add the cooked pasta to the skillet and stir to combine with the chicken. Pour the cheese sauce over the pasta and chicken, stir again, and enjoy!

6. Store any leftovers in an airtight container in the fridge for up to 4 days.

Nutrition (per serving):

CALORIES: 461

TOTAL FAT: 10g

TOTAL CARBOHYDRATE: 47g

PROTEIN: 47g

LEMON-GARLIC CHICKEN WINGS

PREP TIME: 2 hours

COOK TIME: 20 minutes

MAKES: 4 servings

SERVING SIZE: about 4 pieces

2 lb (907g) chicken wings, segmented (about 16–20 pieces)

Olive oil cooking spray

¼ cup grated Parmesan cheese, for topping

For the marinade:

4 garlic cloves, finely minced

¼ cup lemon juice

2 tbsp lemon zest

1 tsp garlic powder

1 tsp salt

1 tbsp paprika

1 tsp black pepper

These wings are made succulent and flavorful by marinating them in a zesty blend of lemon juice, minced garlic, and spices. The lemon juice adds a tangy acidity that cuts through the richness of the chicken, while the garlic enhances the overall depth of flavor. By air-frying or baking these wings instead of frying them in oil, you can reduce the calories and fat significantly.

1. To make the marinade, combine the minced garlic, lemon juice, lemon zest, garlic powder, salt, pepper, and paprika in a small bowl. Whisk to combine.

2. Add the chicken wings to a large bowl. Pour the marinade over the wings, toss to coat, cover, and transfer to the fridge to marinate for at least 2 hours.

3. Preheat an air fryer to 390°F (200°C). Remove the wings from the marinade, place them in a single layer in the fryer, and lightly spray them with olive oil cooking spray. Working in batches if needed, air-fry the wings for 18 to 20 minutes or until crispy, flipping them halfway through the cooking time to ensure both sides cook evenly. (If you don't have an air fryer, you can bake the wings in a 400°F [205°C] oven for 40 to 50 minutes.)

4. Remove the wings from the air fryer, sprinkle with Parmesan, and enjoy.

5. Store any leftovers in an airtight container in the fridge for up to 4 days.

Nutrition (per serving):

CALORIES: 388

TOTAL FAT: 25g

TOTAL CARBOHYDRATE: 2g

PROTEIN: 34g

ITALIAN-STYLE SPAGHETTI SQUASH

PREP TIME: 15 minutes

COOK TIME: 35 minutes

MAKES: 4 servings

SERVING SIZE: ½ spaghetti squash

2 medium spaghetti squash

Salt, to season and taste

Black pepper, to season and taste

1 tbsp olive oil

2 tbsp tomato paste

1 large white onion, chopped

3 garlic cloves, minced

Pinch of crushed red pepper flakes (optional)

1 lb (454g) 95%-lean ground beef

1 (28oz/794g) can crushed tomatoes

1 tbsp onion powder

1 tbsp garlic powder

1 tsp dried oregano

2 bay leaves

Shredded Parmesan cheese, for topping

This is a great lower-carb, fiber-rich pasta alternative; it's healthy, simple, quick, and easy to make, without compromising on flavor. One of my favorite weight-loss hacks is eating lower-calorie but higher-volume foods, and spaghetti squash is a perfect option. Simple substitutions like leaner ground beef help keep the calories and fat on the lower side. This vegetable alternative to traditional pasta still packs as much flavor as its higher-calorie counterpart thanks to the delicious meat sauce made from tomatoes and a blend of traditional Italian seasonings.

1. Preheat the oven to 400°F (205°C).

2. Cut the spaghetti squash lengthwise and then scoop out the seeds. Place the squash, cut sides up, on a baking sheet. Drizzle the cut sides with a small amount of olive oil, then season with salt and pepper.

3. Turn the squash so the cut sides are facing down on the baking sheet. Bake for 30 minutes.

4. While the squash is baking, heat 1 tablespoon of olive oil in a large skillet over medium heat. Add the tomato paste, onion, garlic, and crushed red pepper flakes (if using). Sauté until the onion becomes translucent and fragrant, then add the ground beef. Cook, stirring occasionally and breaking up the beef, until the beef is browned but not cooked all the way through.

5. To the same skillet, add the tomatoes, garlic powder, onion powder, and oregano. Season to taste with additional salt and pepper, then top with the bay leaves. Cover and allow to simmer for 15 minutes.

6. When the squash is done baking, remove it from the oven and run a fork through the flesh to shred the squash into strands. Transfer the squash to 4 separate bowls or use the squash halves as bowls.

7. Discard the bay leaves. Top each serving with equal amounts of the meat sauce, then sprinkle the Parmesan over the top to serve. Store in an airtight container in the fridge for up to 4 days.

Nutrition (per serving):

CALORIES: 463

TOTAL FAT: 13g

TOTAL CARBOHYDRATE: 49g

PROTEIN: 40g

BIG MOMMA BURGERS

PREP TIME: 18 minutes

COOK TIME: 22 minutes

MAKES: 2 burgers

SERVING SIZE: 1 burger

2 tbsp olive oil, divided

1 medium onion, sliced

4 slices turkey bacon

½ lb (227g) 95%-lean ground beef

1 large egg

1 tbsp Worcestershire sauce

1 tsp garlic powder

1 tsp onion powder

1 tsp paprika

1 tsp salt

1 tsp black pepper

2 slices fat-free cheddar cheese

1 medium tomato, sliced

6 pickle slices

2 large iceberg lettuce leaves

2 low-calorie burger buns of your choice

For the Big Momma Burger Sauce:

3 tbsp nonfat Greek yogurt

2 tbsp sugar-free ketchup

1 tbsp prepared mustard

1 tsp garlic powder

1 tsp paprika

1 tsp black pepper

1 tbsp pickle relish

1 tbsp distilled white vinegar

1 tbsp chopped fresh chives

Nutrition (per serving):

CALORIES: 388

TOTAL FAT: 13g

TOTAL CARBOHYDRATE: 26g

PROTEIN: 45g

The burger: an American classic and also a poster child for bad eating habits and obesity. Burgers come with this stigma because they are staples on fast-food menus, but they can be modified to be healthier. This healthier version uses lean ground beef, turkey bacon, and fat-free cheese to cut down on the calories, and it's topped with a delicious classic burger sauce made with healthier, lower-calorie ingredients to help keep you snatched, bestie!

1. Make the Big Momma Burger Sauce by combining all the ingredients in a small bowl and mixing well. Set aside.

2. Heat 1 tablespoon of olive oil in a large skillet over medium heat. Add the onions to the skillet and cook until caramelized. Set the onions aside and place the same skillet back over the heat.

3. Add the turkey bacon slices to the skillet and fully cook. Transfer the bacon to a paper towel–lined plate to drain.

4. In a large bowl, combine the ground beef, egg, Worcestershire sauce, garlic powder, onion powder, paprika, salt, and pepper. Mix well and then divide into 2 patties.

5. Heat the remaining 1 tablespoon of olive oil in the skillet over medium heat. Add the burger patties and fully cook, then add 1 slice of cheddar on top of each patty. Cover the skillet with a lid and allow the cheese to melt for about 1 to 2 minutes.

6. Lightly toast the burger buns until golden brown. Assemble the burgers by adding 1 tablespoon of the Big Momma Burger Sauce to a bottom bun, followed by a lettuce leaf, 1 burger patty, 2 slices of tomato, a spoonful of caramelized onions, 2 slices of turkey bacon, 3 pickle slices, and a burger bun crown. Repeat with the remaining ingredients.

7. Store any leftover sauce in an airtight container in the fridge for up to 4 days.

EASY BEEF BBQ RIBS

PREP TIME: 10 minutes

COOK TIME: 3 hours

MAKES: 1 rack

SERVING SIZE: about 4 ribs

2 tsp salt

2 tsp smoked paprika

2 tsp black pepper

2 tsp onion powder

2 tsp garlic powder

2 tsp cumin

¼ tsp cayenne

2½ lb (1.15kg) rack beef baby back ribs

Sugar-free BBQ sauce of your choice (I use G Hughes Original Sugar-Free BBQ Sauce)

When I started my weight-loss journey, I was determined to make healthier versions of foods that I already enjoyed, and BBQ ribs were no exception. The sugar-free BBQ sauce cuts down on the sugar and calories traditionally associated with BBQ ribs, but without compromising on flavor. They still have that familiar sweet and smoky flavor that we all love.

1. Preheat the oven to 250°F (120°C).

2. In a small mixing bowl, combine the salt, smoked paprika, pepper, onion powder, garlic powder, cumin, and cayenne to make a dry rub.

3. Pat the ribs dry with paper towels. Layer a baking sheet with a large sheet of foil, place the ribs on the foil, then sprinkle the dry rub over both sides of the ribs. Rub the seasonings into the ribs.

4. Wrap the ribs tightly in the foil, ensuring the ribs are completely covered. Bake for 2½ hours.

5. At the 2½ hour mark, remove the ribs from the oven and raise the oven temperature to 400°F (205°C). Remove and discard the aluminum foil, then place the ribs directly onto the baking sheet. Brush the BBQ sauce onto the ribs.

6. Bake the ribs for an additional 15 minutes, then remove them from the oven and allow to rest for 10 to 15 minutes before slicing and serving.

Nutrition (per serving):

CALORIES: 560

TOTAL FAT: 23g

TOTAL CARBOHYDRATE: 5g

PROTEIN: 80g

CHICKEN FAJITA–STUFFED BELL PEPPERS

PREP TIME: 15 minutes

COOK TIME: 45 minutes

MAKES: 2 servings

SERVING SIZE: 4 halves

1 tbsp olive oil

1 medium yellow onion, diced

1 lb (454g) boneless, skinless chicken breast, diced into bite-size pieces

1 tbsp chicken bouillon granules

2 tbsp chili powder

1 tsp cumin

1 tbsp garlic powder

1 tsp paprika

½ tsp salt

1 tsp black pepper

2 large red bell peppers, cut in half lengthwise, seeds and membranes removed

2 large yellow bell peppers, cut in half lengthwise, seeds and membranes removed

¾ cup shredded reduced-fat cheddar cheese

4–5 tbsp finely chopped fresh cilantro

These stuffed peppers are so flavorful and combine the classic flavors of chicken fajitas with the subtle sweetness of red and yellow bell peppers. This delicious, colorful meal is satisfying and packed with protein.

1. Preheat the oven to 375°F (190°C). Line a baking sheet with parchment paper.

2. Add the olive oil to a large skillet over medium heat. When the oil is hot, add the onion and sauté for 2 to 3 minutes.

3. Add the diced chicken breast, bouillon, chili powder, cumin, garlic powder, paprika, salt, and pepper. Stir to combine, reduce the heat to low, cover, and allow to cook about 15 to 20 minutes or until cooked thoroughly.

4. Place the bell pepper halves on the prepared baking sheet. Fill each pepper half with the chicken mixture, then top each half with 1½ tablespoons of the shredded cheese. Bake for 20 minutes or until the cheese is lightly browned. Serve fresh out of the oven, topped with a sprinkling of cilantro.

5. Store any leftovers in an airtight container in the fridge for up to 4 days.

Nutrition (per serving):

CALORIES: 558

TOTAL FAT: 21g

TOTAL CARBOHYDRATE: 1g

PROTEIN: 63g

CARNE ASADA "NACHOS"

PREP TIME: 15 minutes

COOK TIME: 30 minutes

MAKES: 3 servings

SERVING SIZE: ⅓ of nachos

½ cup finely chopped fresh cilantro, plus more for topping

1 small white onion, diced and divided

1 lb (454g) skirt steak

½ tsp salt

1 tsp garlic powder

1 tsp onion powder

1 tsp dried oregano

1 tsp paprika

1 tbsp olive oil

15 mini sweet bell peppers, cut in half lengthwise and seeds, membranes, and stems removed

For the salsa:

3 Roma tomatoes, cut in half

¼ white onion

2 garlic cloves, whole

1 large fresh jalapeño, stem removed

2 fresh guajillo chiles, seeds and stems removed

1 tsp paprika

½ tsp salt

½ tsp cumin

½ tsp chicken bouillon granules

1 tsp black pepper

1 tbsp extra-virgin olive oil

Nutrition (per serving):

CALORIES: 385

TOTAL FAT: 21g

TOTAL CARBOHYDRATE: 13g

PROTEIN: 29g

I love using mini sweet bell peppers for "nachos"—it's one of the hacks that really is a game changer when it comes to volume eating. Not only can you eat more without pushing yourself out of your calorie deficit, you'll be eating your veggies in a tasty and fun way. Mini sweet bell peppers are nutrition powerhouses and contain vitamins A, C, and K, as well as antioxidants.

1. Preheat the oven to 400°F (205°C). Line a rimmed baking sheet with parchment paper.

2. To a large bowl, add the cilantro and half of the diced onion. Toss until combined.

3. To a large bowl, add the skirt steak, cilantro-onion mixture, salt, garlic powder, onion powder, oregano, paprika, and olive oil. Mix until the steak is coated.

4. Preheat a skillet over medium heat. Add the steak and cook to your desired level of doneness. Transfer the cooked steak to a cutting board and let it rest for about 10 minutes before cutting it into small cubes.

5. Place the mini sweet bell peppers cut sides up on the prepared baking sheet. Roast for 15 minutes or until lightly charred.

6. While the peppers are roasting, make the salsa by adding the tomatoes, onion, garlic, jalapeño, and guajillo chiles to a skillet over medium heat. Sauté for 7 minutes or until everything is softened and cooked through. Add to a blender along with the paprika, salt, cumin, chicken bouillon, pepper, and olive oil. Blend until smooth.

7. Once the bell peppers are done roasting, sprinkle the cooked cubed steak on top of the bell peppers, then top with additional chopped cilantro and diced white onion. Drizzle the salsa over the top.

8. Store any leftovers in an airtight container in the fridge for up to 4 days.

BAKED CHICKEN PARM MEATBALLS

PREP TIME: 10 minutes

COOK TIME:
35 minutes

MAKES: 12 meatballs

SERVING SIZE:
4 meatballs

1 lb (454g) ground chicken

1 large egg

1 tbsp garlic powder

1 tbsp onion powder

1 tsp Italian seasoning

½ tsp salt

1 tsp black pepper

¼ cup shredded Parmesan cheese

1 cup reduced-fat shredded mozzarella cheese

2 cups low-sugar marinara sauce (I like Rao's Homemade Marinara Sauce)

This is one of those satisfying meals that makes you forget you're even on a diet. Using ground chicken and reduced-fat mozzarella really makes a difference when you are in a calorie deficit. By using ground chicken instead of traditional fatty ground beef, you cut the calories and fat without compromising protein.

1. Preheat the oven to 400°F (205°C).

2. In a large mixing bowl, combine the ground chicken, egg, garlic powder, onion powder, Italian seasoning, salt, pepper, and Parmesan cheese. Mix well. Use wet hands to shape the mixture into 12 equal-size meatballs.

3. Pour 1 cup of the marinara sauce into a large baking dish, place the meatballs in the sauce, then pour the remaining marinara sauce over the meatballs. Bake uncovered for 30 minutes.

4. Once baked, remove the meatballs from the oven and sprinkle the mozzarella over the top of the meatballs. Switch the oven setting to broil (high).

5. Place the meatballs under the broiler for 4 minutes or until the mozzarella has melted and lightly browned. Serve hot and enjoy.

Nutrition (per serving):

CALORIES: 529

TOTAL FAT: 34g

TOTAL CARBOHYDRATE: 10g

PROTEIN: 45g

NOTES: I love serving this dish with high-protein pasta for those nights when I'm craving traditional Italian spaghetti and meatballs. If desired, you can use a lower-calorie bread to make a meatball parm sub.

CHIPOTLE CHICKEN NACHOS

PREP TIME: 10 minutes

COOK TIME: 16 minutes

MAKES: 6 servings

SERVINGS: ⅙ of nachos

12 low-carb tortillas (I like Mission Low Calorie Yellow Corn Tortillas)

Olive oil cooking spray

1 tsp salt, plus more to season

1 tbsp olive oil

1 lb (454g) ground chicken breast

1 medium yellow onion, chopped

2 tsp chipotle chili powder

2 tsp paprika

1 tsp ground cumin

1 tsp garlic powder

1 tsp crushed red pepper flakes

1 (15oz/425g) can black beans, drained

1½ cups shredded Mexican-blend cheese

Chopped fresh cilantro, for topping (optional)

Diced avocado, for topping (optional)

4 tbsp **Jalapeño-Lime Ranch Dressing** (p. 92) (optional)

I love nachos, and I made all kinds of healthier nacho recipes on my weight-loss journey, but this is one of my favorites. For this recipe, I use lower-calorie corn tortillas and air-fry them to create crispy chips. This result is a combination of crispy, cheesy, spicy, and savory flavors.

1. Preheat the oven to 350°F (175°C).

2. Cut the tortillas into chips and place them on two baking sheets. Lightly spray them with olive oil cooking spray, then lightly sprinkle salt over the top of the chips.

3. Lightly spray the bottom of an air fryer with olive oil cooking spray, then place a single layer of the tortilla chips in the basket. Air-fry, in batches, at 400°F (205°C) for 7 to 8 minutes or until crispy. Repeat until all the chips are cooked. Set aside. (If you don't have an air fryer, you can use an oven to make the chips. Divide them across two baking sheets, spray with olive oil cooking spray, sprinkle with salt, then bake at 375°F [190°C] for 12 minutes or until crispy.)

4. Add the olive oil to a large skillet over medium heat. When the oil is hot, add the ground chicken and onion. Use a wooden spoon to break up the meat. Once the chicken has begun to brown, add the chipotle chili powder, paprika, cumin, 1 teaspoon salt, garlic powder, red pepper flakes, and ¾ cup water. Simmer for 10 minutes or until the liquid in the skillet has thickened slightly and the chicken is fully cooked. Add the black beans, stir to combine, then remove the skillet from the heat.

5. Place the tortilla chips on a baking sheet lined with parchment paper. Spoon the chicken and bean mixture over the nachos, then sprinkle the cheese over the top. Bake for 10 to 15 minutes or until the cheese is melted.

6. If desired, top with the chopped cilantro and diced avocado, then drizzle the Jalapeño-Lime Ranch Dressing over the top.

Nutrition (per serving):

CALORIES: 381

TOTAL FAT: 21g

TOTAL CARBOHYDRATE: 24g

PROTEIN: 24g

TURKEY EGGPLANT LASAGNA

PREP TIME: 20 minutes

COOK TIME: 50 minutes

MAKES: 6 servings

SERVING SIZE: 1 piece

2 medium eggplants

½ tsp salt, plus more for salting

½ tsp black pepper

Olive oil cooking spray

1 large shallot, sliced

2 garlic cloves, minced

1 lb (454g) 94%-lean ground turkey

½ tsp dried oregano

½ tsp paprika

½ tsp chili powder

1 (24oz/680g) jar marinara sauce (I like Rao's Homemade Marinara Sauce), divided

2 cups shredded reduced-fat mozzarella, divided

This recipe is every bit just as delicious as classic lasagna. You know by now that I am not against carbs, and I didn't eliminate them completely during my weight-loss journey, but when it comes to being mindful of calories and portion sizes, you can get more bang for your calorie buck with vegetables. This is one of those recipes that feels like a cheat meal but it isn't!

1. Cut the eggplants lengthwise into ½-inch (1.25cm) slices. (You'll need about 12 slices.) Lay the slices on paper towels and sprinkle each slice with salt. Allow to sit for 15 minutes and then pat any remaining moisture from the slices with paper towels.

2. Preheat the oven to 400°F (205°C). Lightly spray an 8×12-inch (20×30.5cm) baking dish with olive oil cooking spray and set aside.

3. Season the eggplant with the salt and pepper, then spray lightly with olive oil cooking spray. Preheat a large skillet over medium-high heat. Working in batches, add the eggplant slices to the skillet and cook for about 3 minutes or until browned, flipping the slices halfway through the cooking process to ensure both sides are cooked and the slices are slightly browned on both sides. Set aside.

4. Lightly coat the same skillet with additional olive oil cooking spray and then add the sliced shallot and garlic. Sauté for 2 minutes and then add the ground turkey. Season with the oregano, paprika, and chili powder; stir; then add the marinara sauce and stir again. Continue cooking until the turkey is fully cooked, about 12 minutes, using a wooden spoon to break up the meat as it cooks.

5. Add a layer of eggplant slices (about 4) in the bottom of the prepared baking dish. Top with a layer of meat sauce and then a layer of the shredded mozzarella, about ⅓ of each. Add another layer of eggplant slices and then top with another layer of meat sauce and a layer of the mozzarella. Top with a final layer of eggplant slices and the remaining mozzarella. Bake for 35 minutes or until the cheese is bubbly and lightly browned. Cut into 6 equal-size servings.

6. Store any leftovers in an airtight container in the fridge for up to 4 days.

Nutrition (per serving):

CALORIES: 410

TOTAL FAT: 25g

TOTAL CARBOHYDRATE: 19g

PROTEIN: 30g

PESTO SPAGHETTI SQUASH

PREP TIME: 10 minutes

COOK TIME: 45 minutes

MAKES: 2 servings

SERVING SIZE: ½ spaghetti squash

1 medium spaghetti squash
Olive oil cooking spray
12oz (340g) boneless, skinless chicken breasts
½ tsp salt, plus a pinch for seasoning
½ tsp black pepper, plus a pinch for seasoning
½ tsp crushed red pepper flakes
½ cup shredded reduced-fat mozzarella, divided

For the seasoning liquid:
1 tbsp chicken bouillon granules
1 tsp garlic powder
1 tsp onion powder
1 tsp dried oregano

For the pesto sauce:
2 cups fresh basil
2 garlic cloves
½ cup grated Parmesan cheese
1 tbsp extra-virgin olive oil
2 tbsp lemon juice
¼ tsp salt

Nutrition (per serving):

CALORIES: 596
TOTAL FAT: 25g
TOTAL CARBOHYDRATE: 35g
PROTEIN: 60g

You probably feel like you've heard me say this a million times, but when I say volume eating is a lifesaver on a weight-loss journey, please believe me, bestie! And one of my favorite foods for volume eating has to be spaghetti squash. You get a lot of food for fewer calories, which feels like the ultimate cheat code. This pesto spaghetti squash is so flavorful and easy to make!

1. Preheat the oven to 400°F (205°C).

2. Make the seasoning liquid by combining 2 cups of warm water, bouillon, garlic powder, onion powder, and dried oregano in a large bowl. Stir until the bouillon is dissolved. Set aside.

3. Cut the spaghetti squash down the middle lengthwise and scoop out the seeds. Place the halves on a baking sheet. Lightly spray the cut sides with olive oil cooking spray, then season the cut sides with salt and pepper. Turn the squash halves cut sides down on the baking sheet. Bake until the flesh is tender enough to be shredded with a fork, about 40 minutes.

4. While the squash is baking, lightly spray a large skillet with olive oil cooking spray and place the skillet over medium-high heat. When the skillet is hot, add the chicken breasts, season with pinches of salt and pepper, then brown on both sides, about 5 minutes per side. Once the chicken is browned, reduce the heat to medium-low and add 2 cups of the seasoning liquid. Cover and cook the chicken until fully cooked, about 20 minutes. Transfer the chicken to a large bowl and thinly shred with forks. Set aside.

5. Make the pesto sauce by combining the basil, garlic cloves, Parmesan, olive oil, lemon juice, and salt in a blender. Blend until smooth.

6. Once the squash is baked, very carefully remove it from the oven and transfer the halves to a cutting board. Run a fork through the flesh to loosen up the strands. Transfer the squash strands to the same bowl as the shredded chicken, reserving the squash shells. Add the pesto and red pepper flakes. Mix the ingredients until well combined, then divide the mixture evenly between the spaghetti squash shells. Change the oven setting to broil.

7. Top each filled squash shell with ¼ cup shredded mozzarella, then place the squash halves back on the baking sheet and broil for 5 minutes or until the mozzarella is melted and lightly browned.

8. Store any leftovers in an airtight container in the fridge for up to 4 days.

CHICKEN TINGA TOSTADAS WITH SALSA VERDE

PREP TIME: 30 minutes

COOK TIME: 25 minutes

MAKES: 3 servings

SERVING SIZE: 2 tostadas

2 lb (907g) bone-in skinless chicken breasts

1 small white onion, cut into two halves

4 garlic cloves

1 tsp salt

1 tsp black pepper

Olive oil cooking spray

6 yellow corn tortillas (I like Mission brand)

12 tbsp low-fat sour cream

½ head iceberg lettuce, shredded

6 tbsp crumbled queso fresco

1 medium avocado, thinly sliced (optional)

For the salsa verde:

Olive oil cooking spray

10 tomatillos, husks removed

1 garlic clove

2 medium fresh jalapeños, stems and seeds removed

1 small bunch fresh cilantro

2 tsp chicken bouillon granules

I was introduced to this classic Mexican dish by friends, and it has remained one of my favorites. This is a pretty healthy recipe to begin with, but typically the tortilla (tostada) is fried in oil. Now, you know me, friend: If it is normally fried, you had better believe I'm going air-fry or bake it! This is a delicious meal; the chicken is so flavorful thanks to the beautiful green salsa and onion, and you're also getting plenty of protein to help keep you satiated.

1. Add the chicken breasts, 4 cups of water, half of the white onion, garlic cloves, salt, and pepper to a large pot. (If needed, add additional water to ensure the ingredients are just covered.) Cover the pot and place over medium heat. Simmer for 30 minutes or until the chicken is fully cooked. Transfer the chicken from the pot to a cutting board. Use two forks to shred thinly, then set aside. Discard the remaining broth and ingredients.

2. Begin making the salsa verde by lightly coating a medium skillet with olive oil cooking spray. Place the skillet over medium heat. When the skillet is hot, add the tomatillos, garlic clove, and jalapeños. Cook the ingredients while stirring them frequently to ensure they cook and brown evenly, about 10 minutes.

3. Add the tomatillos, garlic clove, jalapeños, cilantro, and chicken bouillon to a blender. Blend until smooth. Set aside.

4. Slice the remaining half of the white onion. Lightly coat a large skillet with olive oil cooking spray and then place the skillet over medium heat. When the skillet is hot, add the sliced onion and sauté for 3 minutes, then add the shredded chicken and salsa verde. Reduce the heat to low and simmer for 5 minutes.

5. Place the tortillas in an air fryer and fry at 400°F (205°C) for about 7 minutes or until the tortillas are crispy. (To bake the tortillas in an oven, lightly coat the tortillas with olive oil cooking spray and bake at 400°F (205°C) for 12 minutes or until crisp, turning them halfway through the cooking time.)

6. Spread 2 tablespoons of the sour cream onto each tostada, followed by one-sixth of the chicken tinga, ¼ cup of the shredded lettuce, 1 tablespoon of the crumbled queso fresco, and 2 thin slices of avocado (if using).

7. Store any leftover chicken tinga and salsa verde in an airtight container in the fridge for up to 4 days.

Nutrition (per serving):

CALORIES: 649

TOTAL FAT: 22g

TOTAL CARBOHYDRATE: 30g

PROTEIN: 80g

PAN-SEARED CHICKEN BREASTS

PREP TIME: 10 minutes

COOK TIME: 20 minutes

MAKES: 4 servings

SERVING SIZE: 2 pieces

4 boneless, skinless chicken breasts (each about 8oz/227g)

¼ tsp salt

1 tsp black pepper

1 tsp onion powder

1 tsp garlic powder

1 tsp dried oregano

1 tbsp chicken bouillon granules

2 tsp paprika

1 tbsp olive oil

Meal-prepped chicken breasts are undeniably one of the key reasons for my weight-loss success. Having meal-prepped chicken breast on hand means I always have something healthy that is ready to eat throughout the week. These chicken breasts are so easy to make, and they pair well with anything: I like to add them to salads, pair them with my favorite veggies, or transform them into chicken salad.

1. Slice each chicken breast in half lengthwise to create 2 slices.

2. In a medium bowl, combine the salt, pepper, onion powder, garlic powder, oregano, chicken bouillon, and paprika. Stir to combine, then season both sides of the chicken breasts with the seasonings.

3. Add the olive oil to a large skillet placed over medium heat. When the oil is hot, add the chicken slices. Lightly brown the slices for 4 minutes per side, then reduce the heat to medium-low and continue cooking for another 15 minutes, turning the pieces every 3 minutes, until fully cooked. (Use a meat thermometer to ensure the internal temperature reaches 165°F [75°C] and they're fully cooked.) Allow the chicken to rest for 5 minutes before serving.

4. Store any leftovers in an airtight container in the fridge for up to 4 days.

Nutrition (per serving):

CALORIES: 315

TOTAL FAT: 10g

TOTAL CARBOHYDRATE: 2g

PROTEIN: 51g

KOREAN CHICKEN TENDERS

PREP TIME: 10 minutes

COOK TIME: 15 to 25 minutes

MAKES: 2 servings

SERVING SIZE: 3 strips

1 cup all-purpose flour

1 tsp garlic powder

1 tsp onion powder

1 tsp salt

1 tsp black pepper

1 tsp cayenne

2 cups Egg Beaters

3 cups corn flakes, lightly crushed

2 (each about 8oz/227g) boneless, skinless chicken breasts, each cut into 3 equal-size strips

Olive oil cooking spray

Sesame seeds (optional, for topping)

¼ cup sliced green onions (optional, for topping)

For the spicy dipping sauce:

¼ cup low-sodium soy sauce

¼ cup water

2 tbsp gochujang paste

1 tbsp rice vinegar

2 tbsp honey

One of the reasons I weighed almost 300 pounds was my love of fried foods. In particular, I loved the crunch that most fried foods have. This recipe uses corn flakes to mimic that delicious crunch, but without all the oil and fat that comes with a piece of fried chicken. I combined my love of fried foods with my love of Korean food in this recipe to come up with the most delicious chicken tenders.

1. Make the spicy dipping sauce by combining the soy sauce, water, gochujang paste, rice vinegar, and honey in a skillet over medium heat. Simmer for 5 minutes or until the sauce has thickened. Set aside.

2. Add the flour, garlic powder, onion powder, salt, pepper, and cayenne to a small bowl. Mix until well combined.

3. Add the Egg Beaters and corn flake crumbs to separate bowls.

4. Dredge the chicken strips in the seasoned flour, then dip them in the Egg Beaters, then press them into the corn flake crumbs to fully coat. Lightly spray the strips with olive oil cooking spray.

5. Air-fry the strips at 350°F (175°C) for 15 to 18 minutes or until the chicken is completely cooked and crispy. (If you don't have an air fryer, lightly spray the chicken with olive oil cooking spray and bake at 400°F [205°C] for 20 to 25 minutes.)

6. Brush the spicy dipping sauce onto the strips. Sprinkle the sesame seeds (if using) and sliced green onions (if using) over the top.

7. Store any leftovers in an airtight container in the fridge for up to 4 days.

Nutrition (per serving):

CALORIES: 381

TOTAL FAT: 3g

TOTAL CARBOHYDRATE: 33g

PROTEIN: 26g

SPICY SALMON TACOS

PREP TIME: 10 minutes
COOK TIME: 12 minutes
MAKES: 2 servings
SERVING SIZE: 2 tacos

Olive oil cooking spray
12oz (340g) skinless salmon filet, cubed
4 yellow corn tortillas (I like Mission brand)
8 tsp crumbled cotija cheese, divided

For the marinade:
2 tbsp low-sodium soy sauce
1 tbsp minced fresh garlic
1 tbsp garlic powder
1 tbsp onion powder
1 tbsp honey
1 tbsp Italian seasoning
1 tsp paprika
¼ tsp stevia
1 tsp lemon pepper
1 tsp Cajun seasoning

For the pico de gallo:
1½ Roma tomatoes, diced
¼ medium red onion, diced
1 cup chopped fresh cilantro, plus more for topping
¼ medium avocado, diced
Juice of 1 medium lime
⅛ tsp salt
⅛ tsp black pepper
⅛ tsp garlic powder

For the spicy mayo sauce:
½ cup light mayonnaise
⅛ cup sriracha
½ tsp hot sesame oil

Nutrition (per serving):
CALORIES: 492
TOTAL FAT: 18g
TOTAL CARBOHYDRATE: 30g
PROTEIN: 41g

If you know me, you know I love tacos, so I had to create a lower-calorie version of traditional salmon tacos. This recipe swaps out the higher-calorie tortillas for a lower-calorie option, swaps the sugar for a natural low-calorie sweetener, and uses light mayo in the sauce to reduce the fat. These simple swaps make a huge difference in the macros but without compromising any flavor.

1. Preheat the broiler to high and adjust a rack about 6 inches (15cm) from the flame. Line a rimmed baking sheet with parchment paper and lightly spray with olive oil cooking spray.

2. Make the marinade by combining the soy sauce, minced garlic, garlic powder, onion powder, honey, Italian seasoning, paprika, stevia, lemon pepper, and Cajun seasoning in a medium bowl. Whisk to combine. Add the salmon, toss to coat, cover, then set aside to marinate for 5 minutes.

3. While the salmon is marinating, make the pico de gallo by combining the tomatoes, onion, cilantro, and avocado in another medium bowl. Gently mix to combine, then add the lime juice, salt, pepper, and garlic powder. Gently mix again, then set aside.

4. Arrange the marinated salmon in a single layer on the prepared baking sheet. Broil for 8 minutes or until the salmon is fully cooked, turning occasionally.

5. While the salmon is broiling, make the spicy mayo sauce by combining the light mayo, sriracha, and hot sesame oil in a small bowl. Mix to combine. Set aside.

6. Preheat a small skillet over medium heat. Place a tortilla on the hot skillet for 2 minutes or until warm and pliable. Repeat with the remaining tortillas.

7. Build your tacos by placing a bed of pico de gallo on a tortilla followed by a quarter of the salmon, a sprinkle of chopped cilantro, a drizzle of the spicy mayo sauce, and 2 teaspoons of cotija cheese. Repeat with the remaining ingredients.

8. Store any leftovers in an airtight container in the fridge for up to 4 days.

SHEET-PAN SALMON AND SWEET POTATOES

PREP TIME: 10 minutes

COOK TIME: 30 minutes

MAKES: 4 servings

SERVING SIZE: 1 salmon filet and ¼ of potatoes and broccoli

Olive oil cooking spray

2 medium sweet potatoes, peeled and diced

2 tsp olive oil

1½ tsp salt, divided

1½ tsp black pepper, divided

4 cups broccoli florets

24oz (680g) salmon fillet, cut into 4 equal-size portions

1 tsp garlic powder

1 tsp onion powder

1 medium lemon, sliced

4 sprigs fresh dill

¼ cup crumbled fat-free feta cheese

I'm a sucker for easy meals, and that's exactly what this recipe is. There's truly nothing better than throwing everything on a sheet pan, baking it, and having dinner ready in 30 minutes. Not only is this recipe quick to prepare, it's healthy—the sweet potato is rich in fiber and nutrients like vitamins A and C, and the salmon offers protein, which is so important to staying satiated on a weight-loss journey.

1. Preheat the oven to 425°F (220°C). Line a rimmed baking sheet with parchment paper and then lightly coat the parchment paper with olive oil cooking spray.

2. Add the potatoes, olive oil, ¼ teaspoon salt, and ¼ teaspoon pepper to a large bowl. Toss the potatoes to coat, then place the potatoes in a single layer on the prepared baking sheet. Roast for 15 minutes.

3. While the potatoes are roasting, add the broccoli florets to the same bowl. Season with ¼ teaspoon salt and ¼ teaspoon black pepper.

4. Season the salmon fillets with the garlic powder, onion powder, remaining 1 teaspoon of salt, and remaining 1 teaspoon of pepper, then spray with olive oil cooking spray.

5. Remove the baking sheet from the oven and move the sweet potatoes to the sides of the sheet. Place the salmon fillets in the center of the baking sheet and then place the broccoli florets around the salmon. Top each salmon fillet with 2 lemon slices and a sprig of dill.

6. Bake for 15 minutes or until the sweet potatoes are tender and the salmon is fully cooked. Top with the crumbled feta and enjoy!

7. Store any leftovers in an airtight container in the fridge for up to 2 days.

Nutrition (per serving):

CALORIES: 381

TOTAL FAT: 19g

TOTAL CARBOHYDRATE: 12g

PROTEIN: 40g

SPICY TURKEY CAULIFLOWER RICE

PREP TIME: 8 minutes

COOK TIME: 20 minutes

MAKES: 2 servings

SERVING SIZE: ½ of rice

1 small head cauliflower, roughly chopped

1 tsp olive oil

8oz (227g) 94%-lean ground turkey

1 medium carrot, peeled and chopped

2 tsp paprika, divided

1 tsp crushed red pepper flakes

1 tsp ground cumin

½ tsp salt

1 tsp black pepper

1 tsp garlic powder

½ red bell pepper, seeded and chopped

½ tsp turmeric

½ tsp chicken bouillon granules

1 tbsp chopped pickled jalapeños

¼ cup sliced green onions, to serve

This is a great high-volume, low-calorie meal option that features a little kick of spice. The lean turkey and cauliflower keep this dish super light on fat, carbs, and calories; it's a quick and easy meal to throw together on those busier nights.

1. Place the cauliflower in a food processor. Process until a rice-like texture is achieved. Set aside.

2. Heat the olive oil in a large skillet over medium heat. When the oil is hot, add the ground turkey, carrot, and ⅓ cup of water. Break up the meat with a wooden spoon, then cover the skillet and cook for 5 minutes. After 5 minutes, add 1 teaspoon of the paprika along with the crushed red pepper flakes, cumin, salt, pepper, and garlic powder. Cook, uncovered, for 3 minutes or until the water has evaporated.

3. Reduce the heat to medium-low and add the bell pepper, cauliflower rice, remaining 1 teaspoon of paprika, turmeric, and chicken bouillon. Stir, cover, and cook for 4 minutes, then remove the lid and add the pickled jalapeños. Stir again and cook for 2 minutes more. Top with the green onions to serve.

4. Store any leftovers in an airtight container in the fridge for up to 4 days.

Nutrition (per serving):

CALORIES: 316

TOTAL FAT: 8g

TOTAL CARBOHYDRATE: 45g

PROTEIN: 33g

GARLIC SHRIMP WITH BROCCOLI

PREP TIME: 5 minutes

COOK TIME: 4 minutes

MAKES: 2 servings

SERVING SIZE: ½ of yield

1 tbsp olive oil

10oz (284g) large shrimp, peeled and deveined

2 cups broccoli florets

3 garlic cloves, minced

1 Roma tomato, diced

1 tbsp lemon juice

2 tbsp reduced-fat cream cheese

⅓ cup arugula

⅓ cup torn fresh basil leaves, plus more for garnish

⅓ cup grated Parmesan cheese, plus more for topping

1 tbsp black pepper

This might be the simplest healthy meal you'll ever make. Being on a weight-loss journey can become overwhelming, especially at the beginning when the lifestyle changes are so new. That's why it's important to have easy meals like this one to make. This recipe is creamy and packed full of flavor from the reduced-fat cream cheese and Parmesan, plus you get protein from the shrimp and fiber from the broccoli.

1. Add the olive oil to a medium skillet over medium heat. When the oil is hot, add the shrimp and broccoli. Cook for 3 minutes or until the shrimp are opaque and the broccoli is tender-crisp.

2. Add the garlic, tomato, lemon juice, and cream cheese. Cook for 1 minute more, then stir in the arugula and basil. Turn off the heat and sprinkle in the Parmesan and pepper. Mix together, sprinkle extra basil leaves over the top, and serve hot.

3. Store any leftovers in an airtight container in the fridge for up to 4 days.

Nutrition (per serving):

CALORIES: 313

TOTAL FAT: 10g

TOTAL CARBOHYDRATE: 8g

PROTEIN: 45g

BEEF AND BROCCOLI STIR-FRY

PREP TIME: 40 minutes

COOK TIME: 10 minutes

MAKES: 3 servings

SERVING SIZE: ⅓ of skillet

3 tbsp coconut aminos (or soy sauce)

½ tsp baking soda

1 tbsp arrowroot flour (or cornstarch)

1 lb (454g) beef flank steak, cut into medium-thin strips

1 tbsp avocado oil, divided

1 garlic clove, minced

2 medium carrots, sliced

1½ cups broccoli florets

1 medium red bell pepper, sliced

3 green onions, chopped

For the stir-fry sauce:

⅓ cup coconut aminos (or soy sauce)

¼ cup beef stock

1 tbsp rice vinegar

2 tsp sesame oil

½ tbsp arrowroot flour (or cornstarch)

I grew up eating Asian takeout and it was one of my favorite unhealthy foods to eat. We all know that Asian takeout is delicious, but unfortunately it's also packed with sugar, sodium, and unhealthy fats; it's also super high in calories. That's being said, when I embarked on making my lifestyle changes, I knew it wasn't going to be sustainable unless I was able to eat the things I enjoyed, and that's where this recipe came into play. It's a much healthier alternative because it has less sodium, sugar, and fat than the takeout version.

1. Make the stir-fry sauce by combining ⅓ cup coconut aminos, beef stock, rice vinegar, sesame oil, and ½ tablespoon arrowroot flour in a microwave-safe bowl. Stir to combine. Set aside.

2. Combine 3 tablespoons coconut aminos, baking soda, and ½ teaspoon arrowroot flour in a medium bowl. Whisk to combine, then add the steak strips and toss to coat. Set aside to marinate for 30 minutes

3. Add 2 teaspoons of the avocado oil to a large skillet or wok over medium-high heat. Add the marinated steak strips and brown the strips (working in batches, if necessary) for 3 minutes or until the desired doneness is achieved. Set aside.

4. Place the skillet back over the heat and add the remaining 1 teaspoon of avocado oil. When the oil is hot, add the garlic and sauté for 30 seconds or just until fragrant. Add the carrots and broccoli, stir, and cook for 3 minutes.

5. Add the bell pepper and cook while continuously stirring for 2 minutes more or until the vegetables are tender-crisp. Add the steak strips to the vegetables and stir to combine. Reduce the heat to low and continue stirring gently until the sauce thickens. Transfer to a serving platter and then sprinkle the green onions over the top.

6. Store any leftovers in an airtight container in the fridge for up to 4 days.

Nutrition (per serving):

CALORIES: 450

TOTAL FAT: 16g

TOTAL CARBOHYDRATE: 34g

PROTEIN: 34g

NOTE: If desired, enjoy served over a bed of rice or over cauliflower rice to keep things lighter.

HONDURAN ENCHILADAS

PREP TIME: 5 minutes

COOK TIME: 45 minutes

MAKES: 4 servings

SERVING SIZE: 2 enchiladas

1 tbsp olive oil

4 tbsp diced green bell pepper

2 tbsp diced red onion

1 garlic clove, minced

2 Roma tomatoes, diced

2 large Yukon Gold potatoes, peeled and diced

1 lb (454g) 93%-lean ground beef

1 cup water, divided

1 tsp garlic powder

2 tsp salt

1 tsp paprika

1 tsp black pepper

½ tsp cumin

1 packet Goya Sazón seasoning (with coriander and annatto)

8 yellow corn tortillas (I like Mission Yellow Corn Tortillas)

¼ medium head white cabbage, thinly shredded

1 medium tomato, thinly sliced

⅓ cup finely grated Parmesan cheese.

For the sauce:

1 tsp olive oil

4 tbsp diced green bell pepper

2 tbsp diced red onion

1 garlic clove, minced

1 (15oz/425g) can tomato sauce

¼ tsp salt

Nutrition (per serving):

CALORIES: 396

TOTAL FAT: 12g

TOTAL CARBOHYDRATE: 22g

PROTEIN: 27g

This recipe takes me back to my childhood: my mom and aunt would make enchiladas for family events as it was an easy and delicious meal to make in large batches. These enchiladas are lower in fat and calories because I use leaner ground beef and air-fried, lower-calorie tortillas. These simple changes reduce the amount of fat and calories, while still keeping the recipe true to its flavor.

1. To make the sauce, add the 1 teaspoon olive oil to a saucepan over medium heat. When the oil is hot, add the bell pepper, onion, and garlic. Stir, then sauté for 2 minutes or until softened. Add the tomato sauce, 1½ cups water, and salt. Stir again, cover, and simmer for 10 minutes, stirring occasionally, then remove from the heat and set aside.

2. Add the olive oil to a medium skillet over medium heat. When the oil is hot, add the bell pepper, onion, garlic, and tomatoes. Sauté for 5 minutes, stirring occasionally, until the onion has softened. Add the potatoes, stir, cover, and cook for 5 minutes more.

3. Add the ground beef and water to the skillet. Use a wooden spoon to break up the meat, then stir to combine the meat with the veggies. Add the garlic powder, salt, paprika, pepper, cumin, and Sazón seasoning. Mix well, then cook, uncovered, for about 10 minutes or until the potato has softened and sauce is thickened. Remove from the heat and set aside.

4. Place the tortillas in an air fryer and air-fry in batches at 400°F (205°C) for about 10 minutes or until the tortillas are crispy. (If you don't have an air fryer, you can bake the tortillas at 350°F [175°C] for 7 to 10 minutes or until crispy, flipping them halfway through the cooking time.)

5. Prepare the enchiladas by placing ¼ cup the seasoned beef onto a tortilla, then topping with a large pinch of the shredded cabbage, 1 tomato slice, 2 tablespoons of the sauce, and a sprinkle of Parmesan. Repeat with the remaining ingredients.

6. Store any leftovers in an airtight container in the fridge for up to 4 days.

NOTE: To ensure the tortillas don't fly around in the air fryer and also come out as flat as possible, place them on the bottom of the air fryer and then place the air-fryer rack on top of them.

BUTTER CHICKEN

PREP TIME: 40 minutes

COOK TIME:
40 minutes

MAKES: 3 servings

SERVING SIZE:
⅓ of skillet

1½ lb (680g) boneless, skinless chicken breasts, cubed

¾ cup plain nonfat Greek yogurt

4½ tsp Kashmiri red chili powder, divided

1 tbsp turmeric powder

1 tsp salt

6 garlic cloves, minced and divided

2 tbsp light butter, divided

1 medium white onion, diced

2 tsp ground cumin

1½ tsp coriander powder

¾ tsp garam masala

1 (28oz/794g) can crushed tomatoes

1 tsp ginger paste

2 tbsp chopped cashews

⅓ cup 2% milk

¼ cup plain nonfat Greek yogurt, for topping (optional)

¼ small bunch chopped fresh cilantro, for topping (optional)

Steamed rice or cauliflower rice, to serve (optional)

This Indian-inspired recipe features chicken simmered in a creamy tomato curry sauce that is packed with spices. The creaminess comes from Greek yogurt, which also adds protein to help keep you feeling full for longer. This version of butter chicken is much lower in calories and fat than traditional butter chicken because of substitutions like light butter, low-fat milk, lean chicken breast, and nonfat Greek yogurt.

1. Combine the chicken, Greek yogurt, 3 teaspoons of the Kashmiri red chili powder, turmeric, salt, and 3 minced garlic cloves in a medium bowl. Stir, cover, and set aside to marinate for 30 minutes.

2. Add the marinated chicken to a large, deep skillet over medium-high heat. Cook the chicken for about 12 minutes, stirring occasionally, until fully cooked, then remove from the skillet. Reduce the heat to medium.

3. To the same skillet, add 1 tablespoon of the butter. When the butter is melted, add the onion and remaining 3 minced garlic cloves. Sauté for 4 minutes or until the onion is softened. Add the cumin and remaining 1½ teaspoons of Kashmiri red chili powder along with the coriander and garam masala. Cook for 1 minute or until fragrant.

4. Add the tomatoes, ginger paste, and cashews. Mix well. Allow to simmer, uncovered, for 15 minutes. Add the sauce to a blender along with the milk and remaining 1 tablespoon of butter. Blend until completely smooth. (Note: leave the top of the blender slightly open to prevent the hot sauce from splattering.)

5. Place the skillet back over medium heat. Add the chicken and blended sauce back to the skillet and bring just to a simmer, then transfer to a serving bowl.

6. Add 2 tablespoons of water to the Greek yogurt (if using). Stir and then drizzle the Greek yogurt over the top of the butter chicken. Sprinkle the cilantro over the top (if using). If desired, serve over steamed rice or cauliflower rice.

7. Store any leftovers in an airtight container in the fridge for up to 4 days.

Nutrition (per serving):

CALORIES: 536

TOTAL FAT: 18g

TOTAL CARBOHYDRATE: 16g

PROTEIN: 76g

TUSCAN CHICKEN PASTA

PREP TIME: 15 minutes

COOK TIME: 30 minutes

MAKES: 4 servings

SERVING SIZE: ¼ of pasta

1½ cups nonfat cottage cheese

¼ cup shredded Parmesan cheese

½ cup nonfat milk

1 tbsp tomato paste

1 tbsp garlic powder, divided

½ tsp crushed red pepper flakes

24 oz (680g) boneless, skinless chicken breasts

2 tsp Cajun seasoning

2 tsp onion powder

2 tsp smoked paprika

1 tsp salt

Olive oil cooking spray

1 large red bell pepper, diced

½ cup diced white onion

1 (6oz/170g) bag baby spinach

8oz (198g) protein pasta, of your choice

½ cup sun-dried tomatoes, drained and chopped

½ cup grated Parmesan cheese, for topping

2 tbsp lemon juice, for topping

Pasta?! While I'm trying to lose weight?! Yes! You can have pasta. My favorite kind of meal is the kind that you would never think of eating when on a diet. I always say anything and everything in moderation. This creamy pasta recipe is packed full of flavor and protein, which will leave you feeling fuller for longer.

1. Combine the cottage cheese, ¼ cup shredded Parmesan, milk, tomato paste, 1½ teaspoons of the garlic powder, and red pepper flakes in a blender. Blend until completely smooth, then set aside.

2. Season the chicken breast with the Cajun seasoning, onion powder, remaining 1½ teaspoons of garlic powder, smoked paprika, and salt.

3. Lightly spray a medium skillet with olive oil cooking spray and place over medium heat. Place the seasoned chicken in the skillet and cook until the internal temperature reaches 165°C (75°C). Transfer the chicken to a cutting board, allow to rest for 5 minutes, then slice and set aside.

4. Wipe the pan clean, lightly spray with olive oil cooking spray, and place over medium heat. Add the bell pepper and onion and cook until soft, about 5 minutes. Add the baby spinach, cover, and allow the spinach to cook, stirring every 2 minutes, until wilted.

5. Cook the pasta according to package directions. Once the pasta is cooked, drain and add it back to the pot. Add the cottage cheese mixture, vegetable mixture, chicken, and sun-dried tomatoes. Stir until everything is well combined. Sprinkle a ½ cup grated Parmesan over the top and then sprinkle the lemon juice over the top.

6. Store any leftovers in an airtight container in the fridge for up to 4 days.

Nutrition (per serving):

CALORIES: 580

TOTAL FAT: 8g

TOTAL CARBOHYDRATE: 53g

PROTEIN: 63g

CHICKEN FRIED RICE

PREP TIME: 15 minutes

COOK TIME: 20 minutes

MAKES: 5 servings

SERVING SIZE: 1¾ cups

1 tbsp garlic powder

5 tbsp low-sodium soy sauce, divided

1 tbsp sriracha sauce, plus more to serve

3 tbsp plus 1 tsp olive oil

25oz (708g) boneless, skinless chicken breast, diced

¾ cup Egg Beaters

3 large eggs

10½ oz (300g) mixed frozen veggies (I use carrots and peas)

3½ cups cold, day-old white rice

2 tbsp sesame oil

This healthier alternative to traditional chicken fried rice is just as delicious as its higher-calorie, higher-fat, higher-sodium counterpart. You can still satisfy your takeout cravings and not compromise on your health journey. This recipe is easy to make and full of veggies and protein.

1. Add the garlic powder, 2 tablespoons of the soy sauce, sriracha, and 3 tablespoons of the olive oil to a large bowl. Whisk to combine. Add the chicken and toss to coat.

2. Place a large nonstick skillet or wok over high heat. Working in two batches, remove the chicken from the marinade and add it to the skillet or wok. Cook until fully cooked, about 15 minutes, stirring occasionally to ensure the chicken cooks evenly. Remove from the skillet and set aside. Wipe the skillet clean.

3. Whisk the Egg Beaters and eggs together in a small bowl. Place the skillet back over the heat. Add the egg mixture to the skillet and scramble, then remove the eggs from the skillet and set aside. Wipe the skillet clean.

4. To the same skillet, add the remaining 1 teaspoon of olive oil, frozen veggies, rice, and chicken. Stir-fry until hot, about 2 minutes.

5. Add the remaining 3 tablespoons of soy sauce and sesame oil to the rice. Stir-fry until hot, about 1 minute more.

6. Store any leftovers in an airtight container in the fridge for up to 4 days.

Nutrition (per serving):

CALORIES: 482

TOTAL FAT: 16g

TOTAL CARBOHYDRATE: 37g

PROTEIN: 44g

CHAPTER 8

LOADED MASHED CAULIFLOWER

PREP TIME: 10 minutes

COOK TIME: 30 minutes

MAKES: 4 servings

SERVING SIZE: ¼ of yield

3 slices turkey bacon

1 large head cauliflower, cut into florets

½ cup low-fat sour cream

1 tsp garlic powder

½ tsp salt

1 tsp black pepper

5 tbsp chopped fresh chives, divided

½ cup reduced-fat shredded cheddar cheese

This recipe was, and continues to be, a staple in my diet. It's perfect for low-calorie volume eating: it's creamy and reminds me of its cousin, loaded mashed potatoes, which was the inspiration for this dish.

1. Add the turkey bacon slices to a medium skillet over medium heat. Cook for 4 to 6 minutes or until crispy. Transfer to a cutting board and chop into small pieces.

2. Add the cauliflower to a large pot and steam over medium heat for 20 minutes or until fully cooked. (Alternatively, you can steam the cauliflower in the microwave on high for 4 to 5 minutes or until fully cooked.) Preheat the oven to 400°F (205°C).

3. Add the steamed cauliflower to a food processor or blender along with the sour cream, garlic powder, salt, and pepper. Blend until completely smooth.

4. Add the mashed cauliflower to a greased 8×8-inch (20×20cm) baking dish. Mix in 3 tablespoons of chopped chives, then top with the cheddar cheese and bacon pieces. Bake for 5 to 10 minutes or until the cheese is melted. Garnish with the remaining 2 tablespoons of chives. Enjoy!

5. Store any leftovers in an airtight container in the fridge for up to 4 days.

Nutrition (per serving):

CALORIES: 117

TOTAL FAT: 3g

TOTAL CARBOHYDRATE: 11g

PROTEIN: 10g

HONDURAN RICE AND BEANS

PREP TIME: 10 minutes

COOK TIME: 20 minutes

MAKES: 4 servings

SERVINGS: 1 cup

1 cup uncooked jasmine rice

1 tbsp olive oil

¼ medium green bell pepper, diced

½ medium white onion, diced

½ tsp salt

1 tsp black pepper

1 tsp chicken bouillon granules

1 (13.5fl oz/400ml) can reduced-fat coconut milk

1 (15oz/425g) can black beans with canning liquid

2 tbsp finely chopped fresh cilantro, for topping (optional)

I grew up eating this dish, as my mom and older sister would make it frequently. Honduran rice and beans, or "arroz con frijoles en coco," has a unique tropical flavor profile that combines the richness of coconut milk with the earthiness of beans and the comforting taste of rice. This version is made lighter than its traditional counterpart by using less oil and swapping in reduced-fat coconut milk for full-fat coconut milk. When it comes to losing weight, I believe anything in moderation is okay. (Rice is not the enemy, and I promise you can still enjoy carbs on a low-calorie deficit.)

1. Rinse the rice under cold water until the water runs clear. Set aside to drain.

2. Heat the olive oil in a medium pot over medium heat. Once the oil is hot, add the bell pepper and onion. Cook for about 3 minutes and then add the rice, salt, pepper, and chicken bouillon. Stir well and allow to cook for about 2 minutes.

3. Add the coconut milk and the black beans along with the canning liquid. Stir to combine, cover, and allow to come to a boil. Once boiling, reduce the heat to low and allow to cook until all the liquid has evaporated and the rice is cooked, about 17 to 20 minutes. Top with chopped cilantro (if using) and then fluff with a fork.

4. Store any leftovers in an airtight container in the fridge for up to 4 days.

Nutrition (per serving):

CALORIES: 355

TOTAL FAT: 11g

TOTAL CARBOHYDRATE: 49g

PROTEIN: 9g

SPICY MARINATED CUCUMBERS

PREP TIME: 10 minutes

COOK TIME: none

MAKES: 2 servings

SERVING SIZE: 1 cup

1 tsp sesame oil

2 tbsp low-sodium soy sauce

2 tbsp rice vinegar

2 tbsp chili crisp oil

Salt, to taste

Black pepper, to taste

2 medium cucumbers, thinly sliced

These marinated cucumbers have a nice kick while still being refreshing. Cucumber is a low-calorie food that was a staple on my weight-loss journey because it allowed for high-volume eating. (The more food I can get for lower calories, the better!) These make a great addition to any meal, but my preferred way is serving them with salmon.

1. Add the sesame oil, soy sauce, rice vinegar, and chili crisp oil to a large bowl. Whisk to combine, then season to taste with salt and pepper.

2. Add the cucumbers to the bowl with the dressing. Toss to coat.

3. Store any leftovers in an airtight container in the fridge for up to 4 days.

Nutrition (per serving):

CALORIES: 180

TOTAL FAT: 13g

TOTAL CARBOHYDRATE: 13g

PROTEIN: 3g

NOT-YOUR-GRANDMA'S COLESLAW

PREP TIME: 5 minutes

COOK TIME: none

MAKES: 6 cups

SERVING SIZE: 1 cup

2 cups shredded red cabbage

2 cups shredded green cabbage

1 cup shredded carrots

½ cup sliced green onions

For the dressing:

⅔ cup plain nonfat Greek yogurt

1 tbsp lemon juice

1 tsp prepared mustard

2 tbsp honey

2 tbsp apple cider vinegar

Salt, to taste

Black pepper, to taste

Traditional coleslaw is swimming in mayonnaise, which makes it super high in calories. Using Greek yogurt in place of mayo makes this classic all-American side dish much lighter. This is easy to throw together and is great for parties and barbecues.

1. Make the dressing by combining the Greek yogurt, lemon juice, mustard, honey, vinegar, salt, and pepper in a large bowl. Whisk until well combined.

2. Add the red cabbage, green cabbage, carrots, and green onions to the bowl with the dressing. Toss until the ingredients are well combined.

3. Store any leftovers in an airtight container in the fridge for up to 4 days.

Nutrition (per serving):

CALORIES: 74

TOTAL FAT: 0g

TOTAL CARBOHYDRATE: 15g

PROTEIN: 4g

CRISPY PARMESAN CARROT FRIES

PREP TIME: 15 minutes

COOK TIME: 30 minutes

MAKES: 3 servings

SERVING SIZE: ⅓ of fries

4 garlic cloves, minced

3 tbsp olive oil

1 tsp paprika

1 tsp salt

1 tsp black pepper

1 lb (454g) large carrots, peeled and cut into fries

⅓ cup grated Parmesan cheese

The Slim Ranch Dip (p. 185), for dipping (optional)

This is an easy side dish to throw together on a busy weeknight. These fries are so full of flavor and offer a fun and healthy alternative to traditional fries, which are full of fat and calories. I promise they'll leave you craving more!

---

1. Preheat the oven to 400°F (205°C). Line a large baking sheet with parchment paper.

2. Add the garlic, olive oil, paprika, salt, and black pepper to a large bowl. Mix well, then add the carrot fries to the bowl. Toss until the fries are fully coated in the seasonings.

3. Spread the carrot fries out in a single layer onto the prepared baking sheet. Sprinkle the Parmesan over the fries. Bake for 25 to 30 minutes, tossing the fries halfway through the cooking time, until the carrots are lightly browned.

4. If desired, serve with The Slim Ranch Dip on the side for dipping.

5. Store any leftovers in an airtight container in the fridge for up to 4 days.

Nutrition (per serving):

CALORIES: 225

TOTAL FAT: 17g

TOTAL CARBOHYDRATE: 16g

PROTEIN: 4g

THE REBEL'S POTATO SALAD

PREP TIME: 20 minutes

COOK TIME: 15 minutes

MAKES: 8 servings

SERVING SIZE: ⅛ of salad

2 tsp salt, divided
1½ lb (680g) medium red potatoes, washed and dried
4 medium eggs

For the dressing:
1 cup plain nonfat Greek yogurt
1 tbsp prepared mustard
¼ cup minced dill pickle
1 tbsp dill pickle juice
⅓ cup minced red onion
⅓ cup minced celery
¼ cup chopped fresh dill
1 tbsp black pepper
1 tsp garlic powder

Potato salads are famously drowning in mayonnaise, but not around these parts, baby. I've swapped out the mayo for plain nonfat Greek yogurt, which lowers the fat and calories. But don't worry, you won't miss the mayo! This potato salad is still very flavorful and creamy.

1. Fill a large pot with water. Add 1 teaspoon of salt and the potatoes, then bring to a boil over high heat. Cook for 15 minutes until fork-tender. Use a slotted spoon to transfer the potatoes to an ice-water bath to cool slightly.

2. Add the eggs to the pot of hot water and cook for 10 minutes.

3. Make the dressing by combining the Greek yogurt, mustard, dill pickle, dill pickle juice, red onion, celery, fresh dill, pepper, garlic powder, and remaining 1 teaspoon of salt in a small bowl. Mix well.

4. Once cooled, dice the potatoes and then peel and chop the eggs. Add to a large bowl.

5. Pour the dressing over the potatoes and eggs. Toss gently until everything is well coated. Refrigerate for 1 hour to cool before serving.

6. Store any leftovers in an airtight container in the fridge for up to 4 days.

Nutrition (per serving):

CALORIES: 116
TOTAL FAT: 3g
TOTAL CARBOHYDRATE: 15g
PROTEIN: 7g

MISO-ROASTED POTATOES

PREP TIME: 15 minutes

COOK TIME: 40 minutes

MAKES: 5 servings

SERVING SIZE: ⅕ of potatoes

6 medium russet potatoes, washed, peeled, and cubed

1 tsp salt, divided

2 tsp chicken bouillon granules

1 tsp black pepper

1 tsp paprika

½ tsp garlic powder

½ tsp onion powder

4 tbsp light butter

1 tbsp white miso paste

6 garlic cloves, minced

The miso in this recipe completely transforms traditional potatoes into a dish that explodes with flavor in every bite. In addition to being super tasty, miso is also very nutritious. It's fermented, which means it's good for your gut, and it's also loaded with minerals and antioxidants.

1. Preheat the oven to 375°F (190°C). Line a baking sheet with parchment paper.

2. Soak the cubed potatoes in cold water for 15 minutes and then rinse until the water runs clear.

3. Fill a large pot with cold water and then season the water with ½ teaspoon of the salt and the chicken bouillon. Bring to a boil over medium-high heat. Once the water is boiling, add the potatoes and boil for 6 minutes or until they have softened slightly.

4. Drain the potatoes in a colander and set them aside to continue draining for 5 minutes. Place the potatoes on the prepared baking sheet, season with the remaining ½ teaspoon of salt, black pepper, paprika, garlic powder, and onion powder. Bake for 30 minutes or until lightly golden, tossing them halfway through the baking time.

5. When the potatoes are almost done baking, add the butter, miso paste, and garlic to a large skillet over medium heat. Sauté until the garlic is slightly golden.

6. Remove the potatoes from the oven. Add them to the skillet and toss to coat. Cook for an additional 10 minutes or until golden brown and crisp.

7. Store any leftovers in an airtight container in the fridge for up to 4 days.

Nutrition (per serving):

CALORIES: 182

TOTAL FAT: 4g

TOTAL CARBOHYDRATE: 33g

PROTEIN: 4g

CHEESY PESTO QUINOA CASSEROLE

PREP TIME: 25 minutes

COOK TIME: 25 minutes

MAKES: 5 servings

SERVING SIZE: ⅕ of casserole

Olive oil cooking spray
1 cup uncooked quinoa
1 lb (454g) fresh broccoli florets, roughly chopped
2 cups sliced button mushrooms
1 cup chopped yellow onion
1 tsp salt, divided
1 tsp black pepper, divided
2 cups low-sodium vegetable broth
1 cup 1% milk
½ cup plain nonfat Greek yogurt
1 cup shredded reduced-fat white cheddar cheese, divided
½ cup grated Parmesan cheese
¼ cup prepared pesto
1 tsp garlic powder
1 tsp crushed red pepper flakes

This delicious casserole is creamy, cheesy, and loaded with broccoli and mushrooms. The Greek yogurt adds creaminess and protein, and the pesto adds loads of flavor. It's everything you would want and more from a casserole!

1. Preheat the oven to 375°F (190°C). Lightly coat a 2½- to 3-quart (2.5- to 3L) baking dish with olive oil cooking spray.

2. Rinse the quinoa through a fine mesh strainer until the water runs clear. Set aside to drain.

3. Lightly spray a large skillet with olive oil cooking spray and place over medium heat. Add the broccoli florets, mushrooms, and onion. Cook until the broccoli is slightly tender and the mushrooms and onions are soft, about 6 minutes. Season with ½ teaspoon of the salt and ½ teaspoon of the pepper. Transfer the broccoli mixture from the skillet to a large bowl. Set aside.

4. To the same skillet, add the drained quinoa, vegetable broth, remaining ½ teaspoon of the salt and remaining ½ teaspoon of the pepper. Bring to a boil, then cover and reduce the heat to low. Simmer for 15 minutes, then turn off the heat, stir, and place the lid back on the pot to steam the quinoa for 5 minutes.

5. After 5 minutes, remove the lid and stir in the milk, Greek yogurt, ½ cup of the shredded cheddar, Parmesan, pesto, garlic powder, and red pepper flakes. Stir to combine, then mix in the broccoli, mushrooms, and onions.

6. Transfer the quinoa mixture to the prepared baking dish and top with the remaining ½ cup of cheddar. Bake for 20 minutes or until the cheese is melted and the mixture is bubbly. Serve hot.

7. Store any leftovers in an airtight container in the fridge for up to 4 days.

Nutrition (per serving):

CALORIES: 391
TOTAL FAT: 16g
TOTAL CARBOHYDRATE: 37g
PROTEIN: 25g

snacks

MANGO PICO DE GALLO

PREP TIME: 15 minutes

COOK TIME: none

MAKES: 10 servings

SERVING SIZE: ½ cup

3 cups diced Roma tomatoes
  (about 4 medium)

1 cup diced white onion

⅓ cup chopped fresh cilantro

1 cup diced ripe mango

¼ cup lime juice

1 tsp garlic powder

1 medium fresh jalapeño, seeds
  removed and minced

Salt, to taste

Black pepper, to taste

This fresh salsa has a sweet and tangy flavor, with a hint of heat from the jalapeño that is balanced by the freshness of the cilantro and the acidity of the lime juice. It's delicious served with tacos, nachos, grilled meats, or as a dip with tortilla chips.

1. Combine the tomatoes, onion, cilantro, mango, lime juice, garlic powder, and jalapeño in a medium bowl. Mix well and then season to taste with salt and pepper.

2. Store in an airtight container in the fridge for up to 4 days.

Nutrition (per serving):

CALORIES: 41

TOTAL FAT: 0g

TOTAL CARBOHYDRATE: 8g

PROTEIN: 0g

THE SLIM RANCH DIP

PREP TIME: 5 minutes

COOK TIME: none

MAKES: 6 servings

SERVING SIZE: 3 tablespoons

1 cup plain nonfat Greek yogurt

1½ tsp garlic powder

1½ tsp onion powder

2 tbsp chopped fresh dill

1 tbsp lemon juice

½ tsp salt

1 tsp Worcestershire sauce

3 tbsp finely chopped fresh chives, for topping (optional)

Ranch is an American staple, but it can also be high in fat and calories. On my weight-loss journey, I would make this healthier ranch dip so that I could snack on veggies throughout the week without guilt. I always say that low-calorie volume eating played a huge role in the success of my weight loss, and this dip definitely helped. This is the perfect healthy dip for any occasion!

1. Add the Greek yogurt, garlic powder, onion powder, dill, lemon juice, salt, and Worcestershire sauce to a medium bowl. Mix until all the ingredients are well combined.

2. Top with the chopped chives (if using). Serve with your favorite veggies like celery, mini sweet bell peppers, carrots, broccoli, or Kale Chips (p. 197).

Nutrition (per serving):

CALORIES: 29

TOTAL FAT: 0g

TOTAL CARBOHYDRATE: 4g

PROTEIN: 4g

BUFFALO CHICKEN DIP

PREP TIME: 10 minutes

COOK TIME: 25 minutes

MAKES: 8 servings

SERVING SIZE: ½ cup

16oz (454g) chicken breast, boneless and skinless

½ white onion

1 tbsp chicken bouillon granules

½ cup low-fat sour cream

⅓ cup hot sauce (I use Frank's RedHot sauce)

1 cup nonfat Greek yogurt

¾ cup shredded reduced-fat cheddar cheese, divided

1 tsp garlic powder

1 tsp black pepper

I'm a huge fan of creating healthier alternatives, and this lower-calorie buffalo chicken dip is a result of that process. During my weight-loss journey, I wanted to have recipes that were just as tasty as their higher-calorie counterparts. This buffalo chicken dip is a perfect example of a recipe that is lower in calories without compromising flavor.

1. Bring a medium saucepan of water to a boil over medium-high heat. Add the chicken breast, onion, and bouillon. Reduce the heat to medium-low and cook, covered, for 25 minutes or until the chicken is cooked through. Remove the chicken from the water and place on a cutting board. Use forks to shred the chicken and then set it aside. Discard the cooking water.

2. Preheat the oven to 350°F (175°C).

3. To a large bowl add the sour cream, hot sauce, and Greek yogurt, and mix well. To the wet ingredients, add the shredded chicken, ½ cup of the cheddar cheese, garlic powder, and pepper. Mix well.

4. Add the mixture to a small baking dish or oven-safe skillet. Top with the remaining ¼ cup of cheddar cheese. Bake for 20 minutes and then broil on high for 2 minutes or until the cheese is lightly browned. Serve with lower-calorie crackers and vegetables on the side for dipping.

Nutrition (per serving):

CALORIES: 124

TOTAL FAT: 3g

TOTAL CARBOHYDRATE: 3g

PROTEIN: 19g

CRUNCHY CHILI-LIME CHICKPEAS

PREP TIME: 5 minutes

COOK TIME: 45 minutes

MAKES: 2 servings

SERVING SIZE: ½ cup

2 tsp olive oil
1 tsp chili powder
¾ tsp salt
¼ tsp black pepper
1 (15.5oz/439g) can chickpeas, drained and rinsed
2 tsp lime zest

These chickpeas (garbanzo beans) are crispy and crunchy and are a flavorful snack on their own or great as a topping for salads. They have a zesty, tangy flavor, with just a hint of heat from the chili powder that is complemented by the brightness of the lime juice.

1. Preheat the oven to 400°F (205°C). Line a rimmed baking sheet with parchment paper.

2. Add the olive oil, chili powder, salt, and pepper to a medium bowl. Whisk to combine.

3. Add the chickpeas to the bowl. Toss to fully coat the chickpeas in the seasonings.

4. Spread the chickpeas in a single layer onto the prepared baking sheet. Bake for 35 to 45 minutes, stirring every 15 minutes, until crispy, sprinkling the lime zest over the chickpeas during the last 5 minutes of baking time.

5. Enjoy as a crunchy snack or add to salads as a topping.

Nutrition (per serving):

CALORIES: 254
TOTAL FAT: 9g
TOTAL CARBOHYDRATE: 34g
PROTEIN: 12g

JALAPEÑO POPPERS

PREP TIME: 10 minutes

COOK TIME: 25 minutes

MAKES: 16 poppers

SERVING SIZE: 4 poppers

5 slices turkey bacon

1 (8oz/226g) package reduced-fat cream cheese

¼ cup reduced-fat plain Greek yogurt

½ cup shredded reduced-fat cheddar cheese

1 tbsp garlic powder

8 large jalapeños (about 1 lb or 454g)

2 tbsp whole-wheat panko breadcrumbs

Olive oil cooking spray

These jalapeño poppers are delicious! I went through a fixation stage with eating these. I love spicy food, and I also love traditional jalapeño poppers, so this healthier version was great for snacking during my weight-loss journey.

1. Preheat the oven to 400°F (205°C).

2. Cook the bacon slices in a skillet over medium heat until crisp, about 8 minutes. Transfer the bacon to a paper towel–lined plate to drain and cool. Once cooled, cut the strips into small bits.

3. In a medium bowl, mix together the cream cheese, Greek yogurt, cheddar cheese, and garlic powder.

4. Cut the jalapeños in half lengthwise, remove the seeds and membranes, and fill each half with the cream cheese mixture. Place the poppers on a baking tray and lightly top with the breadcrumbs and bacon bits. Lightly coat the poppers with olive oil cooking spray.

5. Bake for 10 to 15 minutes or until tender and lightly browned.

Nutrition (per serving):

CALORIES: 203

TOTAL FAT: 13g

TOTAL CARBOHYDRATE: 8g

PROTEIN: 12g

NOTE: You can use an air fryer if you have one. Preheat the air fryer to 375°F (190°C) and air-fry the poppers for about 8 minutes.

PEPPERONI PIZZA BAGELS

PREP TIME: 5 minutes

COOK TIME: 10 minutes

MAKES: 1 serving

SERVING SIZE: 1 bagel

1 low-calorie plain bagel (I like Old Tyme 647), split in half and lightly toasted

3 tbsp low-sugar pizza sauce, divided

½ tsp crushed red pepper flakes

¼ cup shredded reduced-fat mozzarella, divided

10 slices turkey pepperoni, divided

Basil leaves, for garnish

Hands down, this is one the easiest snacks you can whip up. Not only are these easy to make, but they truly taste like something you shouldn't be eating!

1. Preheat the oven to 375°F (190°C). Line a baking sheet with parchment paper.

2. Spread each cut side of the bagel with 1½ tablespoons of the pizza sauce. Sprinkle the red pepper flakes and half of the cheese over the pizza sauce.

3. Top each half with 5 slices of pepperoni and the remaining cheese. Bake for 10 minutes or until the cheese is melted. Top with the basil leaves and enjoy.

Nutrition (per serving):

CALORIES: 312

TOTAL FAT: 8g

TOTAL CARBOHYDRATE: 56g

PROTEIN: 22g

ROASTED GARLIC HUMMUS

PREP TIME: 5 minutes

COOK TIME: 45 minutes

MAKES: 7 servings

SERVING SIZE: 3 tablespoons

1 head garlic

1 tsp extra-virgin olive oil, plus more for drizzling

½ tsp salt, plus extra for seasoning

1 (15.5oz/439g) can chickpeas, drained and rinsed

2 tbsp tahini

3 tbsp lemon juice

This hummus is one of my all-time favorite dips! I meal prepped a lot of foods on my journey so that I would always have healthy food options available, and this hummus was one of the recipes I always added to my meal-prep snack boxes. It's an excellent source of healthy fats, protein, and fiber.

1. Preheat the oven to 400°F (205°C). Prepare the garlic by cutting off the very top of the head so that most of the cloves are exposed. Wrap the garlic head in tin foil, leaving an opening in the foil so the tops of the cloves are exposed to the heat. Drizzle the olive oil over the head and then lightly sprinkle some salt over the top. Bake for 40 to 45 minutes or until the garlic cloves are soft and golden brown.

2. To a food processor or blender, add the chickpeas, ¼ cup warm water, tahini, ½ teaspoon salt, and lemon juice. Squeeze the garlic head to transfer the roasted cloves to the food processor or blender. Blend until smooth. If desired, top with a drizzle of olive oil before serving.

3. Store any leftovers in an airtight container in the fridge for up to 4 days.

Nutrition (per serving):

CALORIES: 141

TOTAL FAT: 7g

TOTAL CARBOHYDRATE: 16g

PROTEIN: 5g

NOTES: Serve with warm pita bread, crispy bread, carrots, radishes, cucumber, or sweet mini bell peppers.

HAM-AND-CHEESE POCKETS

PREP TIME: 7 minutes

COOK TIME: 4 minutes

MAKES: 2 servings

SERVING SIZE:
4 pockets

2 lavash breads (flatbreads)

2oz (55g) thinly sliced turkey ham

⅓ cup low-fat cottage cheese

½ cup reduced-fat cheddar cheese

½ tsp garlic powder

I'm a big texture person, so I love a good crunch in my food. These cheesy, high-protein, low-calorie snacks are easy to make and will kick your cravings for something crunchy. They're gooey and cheesy on the inside, and crunchy on the outside.

1. Cut each lavash bread lengthwise into 2 slices.

2. Cut the turkey ham slices into small pieces and then add to a medium bowl. Add the cottage cheese, cheddar cheese, and garlic powder. Mix well.

3. To one lavash, add 1 tablespoon of the filling toward the bottom of the bread. Pull the corners together to fold the bread into a triangle, then pinch the edges shut.

4. Place the pockets seam sides down in an air fryer and cook at 400°F (205°C) for 3 to 4 minutes.

Nutrition (per serving):

CALORIES: 229

TOTAL FAT: 6g

TOTAL CARBOHYDRATE: 18g

PROTEIN: 29g

NOTE: If you don't own an air fryer, you can bake these in the oven at 400°F (205°C) for 6 to 10 minutes. (Just keep a close eye on them, as the flatbreads are thin and can burn easily.)

KALE CHIPS

PREP TIME: 10 minutes

COOK TIME:
20 minutes

MAKES: 2 servings

SERVING SIZE:
½ of chips

1 large bunch kale
1 tbsp olive oil
1 tsp flaked sea salt

Kale chips are a classic, healthy snack. They are nutritious, super easy to make, and will help curb those snacking cravings. I love a good crunchy snack, and I just love the act of eating, which is what got me to almost 300 pounds. So these kale chips came to the rescue as it's a low-calorie snack that I can have throughout the day without jeopardizing my progress.

1. Preheat the oven to 300°F (150°C). Line a baking sheet with parchment paper.

2. Remove the kale leaves from the stems. Wash and dry the leaves and then tear them into small bite-size pieces.

3. To a large bowl, add in the kale and then drizzle in the olive oil. Toss to mix well.

4. Spread the kale out onto the prepared baking sheet and then sprinkle with the sea salt.

5. Bake for 20 to 30 minutes or until the leaves just begin to brown.

6. Enjoy your chips without any regrets!

Nutrition (per serving):

CALORIES: 109
TOTAL FAT: 4g
TOTAL CARBOHYDRATE: 9g
PROTEIN: 8g

NOTE: Be very careful not to let the kale burn. It is expected that some leaves will start to brown, which is when you should remove the kale chips from the oven.

DES

GUILT-FREE BROWNIES

PREP TIME: 5 minutes

COOK TIME:
20 minutes

MAKES: 6 servings

SERVING SIZE:
1 brownie

½ cup rolled oats

¼ cup unsweetened cocoa powder

½ tsp ground cinnamon

1 tbsp baking powder

⅓ cup plain nonfat Greek yogurt

¼ cup stevia

1 large egg

¼ cup plain unsweetened almond milk

2 tbsp chocolate chips (about 30 chips), for topping (optional)

Chocolate is my ultimate weakness, so brownies have always been one of my go-to desserts. And since I didn't want to cut out the things that brought me pleasure and happiness, I realized I had to create a healthier brownie recipe. This recipe uses oat flour, which makes these brownies rich in fiber, while Greek yogurt adds protein, and stevia keeps them low in sugar.

1. Preheat the oven to 400°F (205°C).

2. Process the oats in a food processor or blender until a flourlike consistency is achieved.

3. Combine the processed oats, cocoa powder, cinnamon, baking powder, Greek yogurt, stevia, egg, and almond milk in a large bowl. Mix well.

4. Pour the batter into an 8-inch (20cm) square baking pan. Top with the chocolate chips (if using). Bake for 15 to 20 minutes or until a toothpick inserted into the center comes out clean. Cut into 6 equal-size servings.

5. Store any leftovers in an airtight container in the fridge for up to 4 days.

Nutrition (per serving):

CALORIES: 72

TOTAL FAT: 3g

TOTAL CARBOHYDRATE: 10g

PROTEIN: 4g

CHOCOLATE-STRAWBERRY YOGURT BARK

PREP TIME:
2 hours 10 minutes

COOK TIME: none

MAKES: about
8 servings

SERVING SIZE: 1 piece

1½ cups nonfat plain
  Greek yogurt
1 tbsp vanilla extract
1 tbsp stevia (adjust amount
  depending on how sweet
  you prefer)
1 (3.5oz/100g) 70% cocoa
  chocolate bar (I like Lindt
  brand)
2 cups diced fresh
  strawberries
¼ cup sliced raw almonds

This yogurt bark offers a delightful combination of creamy, tangy, chocolaty, and sweet flavors, which together make this sweet treat the perfect combination of light and indulgent. The base of the bark is made from nonfat plain Greek yogurt, which packs this dessert with protein.

1. Add the Greek yogurt, vanilla extract, and stevia to a medium bowl. Mix well to combine.

2. Line a rimmed baking sheet with parchment paper. Spread the yogurt evenly over the parchment paper.

3. Break the chocolate into pieces, place the pieces in a microwave-safe bowl and microwave in 15-second intervals, removing the chocolate from the microwave at each interval and stirring, until the chocolate is completely melted and smooth.

4. Spoon the chocolate over top of the Greek yogurt and then gently run a kitchen knife over the dollops of chocolate to create a wave pattern throughout the yogurt.

5. Top with the diced strawberries and chopped almonds. Place in the freezer for at least 2 hours or until firm. Use a sharp knife to cut the bark into 8 equal-size pieces.

6. Store in an airtight container or bag in the freezer for up to 3 months.

Nutrition (per serving):

CALORIES: 126
TOTAL FAT: 7g
TOTAL CARBOHYDRATE: 12g
PROTEIN: 6g

GREEK YOGURT CHEESECAKE WITH RASPBERRY SAUCE

PREP TIME: 7 hours

COOK TIME: 1 hour 5 minutes

MAKES: 10 slices

SERVING SIZE: 1 slice

For the crust:

1 cup rolled oats

1 egg white

3 tbsp honey

For the filling:

2 cups plain nonfat Greek yogurt

8 oz (227g) reduced-fat cream cheese, softened to room temperature

1 tsp baking powder

1 tsp vanilla extract

3 tbsp stevia

For the raspberry sauce:

1½ cups fresh raspberries, plus more for topping

1 tbsp honey

1 tsp vanilla extract

2 tsp cornstarch

When I learned you can use Greek yogurt to make cheesecake, my mind was blown! Not only does it create a healthier cheesecake, but it actually tastes good! This is a delicious, lighter dessert option that will help you satisfy those cheesecake cravings without derailing your journey.

1. Preheat the oven to 325°F (165°C). Grease a 9-inch (23cm) pie pan.

2. Process the oats in a food processor or blender until a flourlike consistency is achieved. Combine the processed oats, egg white, and honey in a medium bowl. Mix until a dough is formed.

3. Add the dough to the pan and spread it out thinly on the bottom of the pan to form a crust. Place the crust in the fridge while you make the cheesecake filling.

4. Make the filling by combining the Greek yogurt, cream cheese, baking powder, vanilla extract, and stevia in a medium bowl. Mix until completely smooth, then transfer the filling to the pie pan.

5. Add 6 cups of water to a large saucepan placed over high heat. Bring the water to a boil, then very carefully transfer the water to a large baking dish. Place the water-filled baking dish on the middle oven rack.

6. Place the prepared cheesecake on the top oven rack. Bake for 20 minutes, then reduce the oven temperature to 200°F (95°C). Bake for 45 minutes more or until the center is set. (The middle should jiggle slightly, like gelatin, but still be firm.) Once the cheesecake is baked, turn off the oven, crack the oven door, and let the cheesecake cool in the oven for 1 hour before transferring to the fridge to chill for 6 hours.

7. Make the raspberry sauce by adding the raspberries, ¼ cup of water, and honey to a small saucepan. Stir, then bring the mixture to a boil over medium-high heat. Once the mixture is boiling, reduce the heat to low and use a potato masher to crush the raspberries. Add the vanilla extract, stir, and allow to simmer for 5 minutes more.

Nutrition (per serving):

CALORIES: 96

TOTAL FAT: 3g

TOTAL CARBOHYDRATE: 9g

PROTEIN: 8g

8. Mix the cornstarch and another ¼ cup of water into a slurry and stir into the hot berry mixture. Simmer for an additional 5 minutes, then strain the sauce through a fine mesh strainer and into a bowl.

9. When you're ready to serve, drizzle each slice with the raspberry sauce and then top each slice with a few raspberries.

10. Store any leftovers in an airtight container in the fridge for up to 4 days.

RASPBERRY-CHOCOLATE BARS

PREP TIME:
2 hours 30 minutes

COOK TIME: none

MAKES: 8 servings

SERVING SIZE: 1 slice

4 thin plain rice cakes, crumbled

1 (3.5oz/100g) bar 70% cocoa dark chocolate, divided (I use Lindt brand)

¼ cup powdered peanut butter (I like PBfit brand)

¼ cup almond milk (or milk of your choice)

Sea salt, for topping

For the filling:

1 cup fresh raspberries

2 tbsp chia seeds

1 tbsp honey

While I was on my journey, I discovered how versatile rice cakes could be for making snacks and desserts. These bars offer the perfect balance of textures and flavors; the crispiness of the rice cakes contrasts beautifully with the soft and fruity raspberry filling.

1. Place ¾ of the chocolate in a microwave-safe bowl. Microwave in 15-second intervals while frequently removing the chocolate from the microwave and stirring until the chocolate is completely melted and smooth.

2. Add the powdered peanut butter and almond milk to the bowl with the chocolate. Mix until well combined, then add the crumbled rice cakes and stir again to combine. Transfer the mixture to a 5×9.5-inch (13×24cm) loaf pan lined with parchment paper and then transfer to the fridge while you make the raspberry filling.

3. To make the filling, combine the raspberries, chia seeds, honey, and 1 tablesooon water in a medium bowl. Use a fork to mash the ingredients until a jamlike texture is achieved. Set aside for 20 minutes to thicken.

4. Once the raspberry mixture has thickened, remove the rice cake base from the fridge. Spread the raspberry mixture evenly over top of the rice cake base. Melt the remaining ¼ of the dark chocolate bar and then spread it over the jam. Lightly sprinkle the sea salt over the top and then place the pan back in the refrigerator for at least 2 hours to firm up.

5. Once the bars are set, remove the pan from the freezer and remove the bar from the pan. Cut into 8 equal-size slices. Store in the freezer in an airtight container or bag for up to 2 months.

Nutrition (per serving):

CALORIES: 165

TOTAL FAT: 9g

TOTAL CARBOHYDRATE: 18g

PROTEIN: 4g

CHOCOLATE PUDDING

PREP TIME: 7 minutes

COOK TIME:
10 minutes

MAKES: 3 servings

SERVING SIZE: 1 cup

3 tbsp cornstarch

2½ cups unsweetened almond milk (or milk of your choice), divided

¼ tsp salt

¼ cup unsweetened cocoa powder

⅓ cup erythritol

¾ tsp vanilla extract

3.5oz (85g) 70% cocoa chocolate bar, chopped (I like Lindt brand)

Mixed berries, for topping (optional)

This dessert is made from healthier ingredients to reduce the added sugar and fat that traditional chocolate pudding contains. The cocoa powder provides a rich and intense chocolate flavor, the almond milk adds a subtle creaminess, and the natural sweetener makes it sweet without the blood sugar spikes that can come from a traditional pudding.

1. In a small bowl, combine the cornstarch and ½ cup of the almond milk. Whisk until the cornstarch is completely dissolved. Set aside.

2. Combine the salt, cocoa powder, erythritol, and remaining 2 cups of almond milk in a medium saucepan over medium heat.

3. Stir the cornstarch mixture again and then add it to the saucepan. Bring to a boil while whisking continuously for 2 to 3 minutes, then reduce the heat to low. Simmer for 1 minute more and then turn off the heat.

4. Stir in the vanilla extract and chopped chocolate. Stir continuously until the chocolate is completely melted and incorporated into the mixture.

5. Transfer the mixture to a container, cover, and place in the fridge for a minimum of 4 hours or up to overnight to set. Once the mixture is set, scoop it into individual serving dishes and then top with berries (if using).

6. Store any leftovers in an airtight container in the fridge for up to 4 days.

Nutrition (per serving):

CALORIES: 266

TOTAL FAT: 14g

TOTAL CARBOHYDRATE: 28g

PROTEIN: 4g

NOTE: Erythritol is a natural sweetener that is plant derived. If you prefer not to use erythritol, you can substitute an equal amount of honey or maple syrup.

SIN-FREE CARROT CAKE

PREP TIME: 10 minutes

COOK TIME: 45 minutes

MAKES: 12 servings

SERVINGS SIZE: 1 slice

2 large eggs

½ cup zero-calorie brown sugar replacement sweetener (I use Swerve brand)

¼ cup unsweetened applesauce

1 cup nonfat plain Greek yogurt

1 tsp vanilla extract

1 cup all-purpose flour

2 tsp baking powder

½ tsp salt

1 tsp ground cinnamon, plus extra for dusting

1 tsp ground ginger

1 cup grated carrot (about 2 medium carrots)

¼ cup walnuts, chopped (optional)

Olive oil cooking spray

For the cream cheese frosting:

8oz (227g) reduced-fat cream cheese, softened to room temperature

¼ cup plain nonfat Greek yogurt

¼ cup zero-calorie brown sugar replacement sweetener (I use Swerve brand)

1 tsp vanilla extract

Nutrition (per serving):

CALORIES: 170

TOTAL FAT: 10g

TOTAL CARBOHYDRATE: 19g

PROTEIN: 7g

This carrot cake recipe is lower in calories, sugar, and carbs in comparison to traditional carrot cake. It uses protein-packed swaps that result in a larger serving that is much healthier than its traditional counterpart.

1. Preheat the oven to 350°F (175°C).

2. In a medium bowl, whisk the eggs and ½ cup brown sugar sweetener until a light and fluffy consistency is achieved. Gently fold in the applesauce, 1 cup Greek yogurt, and vanilla extract. Set aside.

3. In a separate bowl, combine the flour, baking powder, salt, cinnamon, and ginger. Stir to combine.

4. Add the dry ingredients to the wet ingredients and mix until well combined. Fold in the grated carrots and chopped walnuts (if using).

5. Spray two 6-inch (15cm) round cake pans with olive oil cooking spray. Pour the batter into the pans. Bake for 20 minutes or until a toothpick inserted into the center comes out clean. Once the cakes are done baking, set them aside to cool completely in the pans.

6. While the cakes are cooling, make the cream cheese frosting. In a large bowl, combine the cream cheese, ¼ cup Greek yogurt, ¼ cup brown sugar sweetener, and vanilla extract. Whisk until a smooth and fluffy consistency is achieved, about 4 minutes.

7. Once the cakes have cooled completely, remove them from the baking pans. Cover the top of one cake with ½ cup of the frosting, then place the other cake on top of the frosted cake. Top with the remaining frosting and then dust with extra cinnamon, if desired. Slice to serve.

8. Store any leftovers in an airtight container in the freezer for up to 3 months.

OAT CHOCOLATE CHIP COOKIES

PREP TIME: 15 minutes

COOK TIME: 15 minutes

MAKES: 16 servings

SERVING SIZE: 1 cookie

¼ cup coconut oil, melted
3 tbsp stevia
2 large eggs
1 tsp vanilla extract
1 cup quick oats
¾ cup whole wheat flour
1 tsp baking powder
Pinch of salt
½ cup dark chocolate chips

These delicious treats combine the heartiness of oats with the indulgent sweetness of dark chocolate chips. This recipe does not include unhealthy sugars; instead, a natural sweetener is used to keep it light. These cookies are packed with essential nutrients, protein, and fiber.

1. Preheat the oven to 350°F (175°C). Line 1 large baking sheet with parchment paper.

2. Add the coconut oil, stevia, eggs, and vanilla extract to a small bowl. Mix until the ingredients are well combined.

3. Add the oats, flour, baking powder, and salt to a medium bowl. Mix to combine.

4. Add the wet ingredients to the dry ingredients and mix until well combined. Use a spatula to gently fold in the chocolate chips.

5. Roll rounded tablespoons of the dough into balls. Place the balls on the prepared cookie sheet about 2 inches (5cm) apart, then flatten them slightly with the back of a spoon. Bake for 12 to 15 minutes or until golden brown.

6. Store any leftovers at room temperature for up to 4 days.

Nutrition (per serving):

CALORIES: 87
TOTAL FAT: 5g
TOTAL CARBOHYDRATE: 10g
PROTEIN: 2g

LEAN MACHINE BANANA BREAD

PREP TIME: 10 minutes

COOK TIME:
35 minutes

MAKES: 8 servings

SERVING SIZE: 1 slice

4 ripe medium bananas
2 cups rolled oats
 (about 1½ cups oat flour)
2 large eggs
⅓ cup plus 1 tbsp honey
¼ cup nonfat plain Greek
 yogurt
2 tsp vanilla extract
1 tsp ground cinnamon
1 tsp baking soda
Pinch of salt

I think we can all agree that if you don't like banana bread, you're psychotic! Banana bread is one of those classic all-American comfort foods that just makes your day better. This banana bread is made with oat flour, which makes it rich and fiber and also means it has a lower glycemic index, reducing the risk of insulin resistance.

1. Preheat the oven to 350°F (175°C). Line a 9×5-inch (23×13cm) loaf pan with parchment paper and then grease the pan.

2. To a medium bowl, add the bananas and mash using a potato masher or fork, until almost smooth.

3. Process the oats in a food processor or blender until a flourlike consistency is achieved.

4. Add the oat flour, eggs, honey, yogurt, vanilla extract, cinnamon, baking soda, and salt to the mashed banana; mix well to combine. Scrape the batter into the prepared pan.

5. Bake for 35 minutes or until a toothpick inserted into the center comes out clean. Transfer the bread to a wire rack and let it cool for 10 minutes before cutting it into 8 slices.

6. Store any leftovers in an airtight container in the fridge for up to 4 days.

Nutrition (per serving):

CALORIES: 198
TOTAL FAT: 4g
TOTAL CARBOHYDRATE: 67g
PROTEIN: 9g

QUINOA ARROZ CON LECHE

PREP TIME: 10 minutes

COOK TIME: 20 minutes

MAKES: 4 servings

SERVING SIZE: ½ cup

1 medium lemon

½ cup uncooked quinoa

1 (13.5oz/400ml) can reduced-fat coconut milk

½ cup plain unsweetened almond milk

2 cinnamon sticks

1 tbsp vanilla extract

1 tbsp stevia, plus more to taste

Ground cinnamon, for dusting

This recipe reminds me so much of my mom and my childhood. My family is Honduran and Salvadoran, and *arroz con leche* (rice pudding) is a staple for many families in Latin America. It's one of my favorite sweet treats, so I just knew I had to come up with a healthier alternative.

1. Peel the rind from the lemon, making sure to avoid the bitter white part (pith). Set aside.

2. Rinse the quinoa repeatedly until the water runs clear.

3. Add 1 cup of water and the quinoa to a medium saucepan. Bring to a boil, then reduce the heat to low, cover, and cook for 10 minutes. Once the quinoa is cooked, remove from the heat and strain through a fine mesh strainer.

4. To a second saucepan, add the coconut milk, almond milk, cinnamon sticks, lemon peel, cooked quinoa, vanilla extract, and stevia. Cover, bring to a boil, then reduce the heat to medium-low. Simmer for 10 minutes or until thick and creamy.

5. Remove and discard the cinnamon sticks and lemon peel, allow to rest for 5 minutes, then dust with ground cinnamon. Enjoy!

Nutrition (per serving):

CALORIES: 160

TOTAL FAT: 8g

TOTAL CARBOHYDRATE: 16g

PROTEIN: 4g

NOTES: This treat can be eaten either cold or hot; it just comes down to personal preference. If you want a thinner consistency, simmer the pudding for less time, but keep in mind that once the pudding has cooled it will absorb the liquid and thicken even more.

INDEX

ABOUT THE AUTHOR

Benji Xavier is a TikTok and Instagram star who made a name for himself by losing over 100 pounds while eating in a more sustainable, less restrictive way. Benji discovered that you can achieve a healthier weight by cooking delicious recipes that substitute less healthy ingredients for healthier ingredients; he believes you can still eat the foods you love, but without making yourself miserable in the process. Benji has nearly 5 million followers across his social media channels who all look forward to his healthy cooking videos each week as they embark on their own healthy weight-loss journeys. Find Benji on TikTok (@benjixavier), Instagram (benjixavierr), and YouTube (@benjixavier).